on track ...

Oasis

every album, every song

Andrew Rooney

sonicbondpublishing.com

Sonicbond Publishing Limited
www.sonicbondpublishing.co.uk
Email: info@sonicbondpublishing.co.uk

First Published in the United Kingdom 2023
First Published in the United States 2023

British Library Cataloguing in Publication Data:
A Catalogue record for this book is available from the British Library

ISBN 978-1-78952-300-3

Typeset in ITC Garamond Std & ITC Avant Garde Gothic
Printed and bound in England

Graphic design and typesetting: Full Moon Media

Follow us on social media:
Twitter: https://twitter.com/SonicbondP
Instagram: www.instagram.com/sonicbondpublishing_/
Facebook: www.facebook.com/SonicbondPublishing/

Linktree QR code:

Acknowledgements

I would like to express my gratitude to Stephen Lambe for giving me the opportunity to write this book, as well as the behind-the-scenes editors who make the wheels turn.

Thanks to my dad, Jack, who was the first person to mention Definitely Maybe to me and to my mom, Patti, who eventually bought it for me when I finally appreciated its greatness. Thanks to Olivia for loving books even more than I do and always inspiring me to be my best self.

I dedicate this book to Lorraine. Thank you for your constant encouragement, support and love. I couldn't have done this without you.

And to Noel, thank you for these songs.

on track ...

Oasis

Contents

Introduction: Manchester, Rain And Noel

Noel Gallagher has always been seen as *the* songwriter in Oasis, but people often forget that the band was formed before Noel joined. Noel Gallagher – eventually called The Chief – and the architect of the Oasis sound, was born on 29 May 1967. As he would recall:

> *Sgt. Pepper* came out on 1 June and, I do believe, on hospital radio, they were playing *Sgt. Pepper* as I was born into the world, and if that's not fucking true, that's the story I've been sticking to for the past 48 years.

His parents, Peggie 'or Peggy' and Tommy, had an older son, Paul, and then the youngest, Liam, would be born five and half years later on 21 September 1972. The kids spent most of their childhood in the Manchester suburb of Burnage, with Noel and Liam sharing a bedroom for a good chunk of that time. Their age difference, however, prevented any type of real closeness from ever forming.

> I didn't hang around with Liam until I joined the band. Although I shared a room with him, five years is a generation apart… I'm leaving school at 15, he's ten years old. You're fucking smoking weed at 15, he's just out of short pants, so there is no relationship.

Neither Noel nor Liam Gallagher being built for traditional jobs, Noel discovered weed, The Smiths, The Jam and realised that everything he could ever want was coming out of those speakers. He quickly began developing his songwriting chops, before landing a job as a roadie/tech with the Inspiral Carpets, which lasted until 1991. Liam, realising he had a voice, and already effortlessly exuding cool, became obsessed with the idea of being in a rock 'n' roll band and found himself singing for a group called The Rain, who had just sacked their first singer and invited Liam to audition. However, Liam claims he was never *in* The Rain, as he tells it:

> So, they liked it and then they went, 'Right, look, do you want to be in this band?' I says, 'Yeah, but we'll have to change that fucking name though 'cause it's terrible', and we changed it to Oasis and that was it. So, for the record, I was never in a band called The Rain.

Liam knew he was going to be famous, he knew he was cool and he knew he could sing. However, he also knew he was not a songwriter and he needed someone to write the songs. At this point, Oasis included Liam on vocals, Paul Arthurs (or Bonehead) on guitar, Paul McGuigan (or Guigsy) on bass and Tony McCarroll on drums. While recollections differ slightly, there are generally considered to be three songs recorded by Oasis that do not include Noel, all collected on a single tape, recorded at Out Of The Blue Studios. The line-up listed on the cassette itself shows Noel as playing Rythm 'not a typo', but Tony McCarroll writes in his book *Oasis: The Truth – My Life As Oasis' Drummer*, that this session was done before Noel joined and that the demo was done for free in exchange for free plastering work, which was apparently a speciality of McCarroll. There was also a phone number left on the cassette: 'For Info Ring 442-1107!'

Author Note

When timings on a song are mentioned, I am going off of Spotify timings. Almost every song discussed in this book can be accessed on streaming services, as most of these services made the vast majority of Oasis singles available last year, making it incredibly easy to be an Oasis fan. Granted, this takes away some of the romanticism surrounding collecting Oasis singles. During the height of the CD era in the 1990s and early noughties, it was always difficult to hear B-sides unavailable on *The Masterplan* without purchasing the often very expensive Oasis singles. There was a joy and an art in this pursuit, as journalist Steven Hyden has spoken of. Tracking down the 'Cigarettes & Alcohol' single, say, always carried an inherent joy and, somehow, the songs sounded even better when heard in that context. This also created a scenario whereby all but the most devoted of fans, especially in America, never heard even semi-obscure songs tucked away on the dozens of singles that have been released since 1994. This current author spent hundreds upon hundreds of dollars buying used copies of every Oasis single, with the Japanese import of 'Don't Go Away' always being especially expensive and tough to find. They are still proudly displayed on top of a CD shelf that does not get much use these days. But now, any fan can make an Oasis playlist that includes almost any and all B-sides, demos, outtakes, live tracks, etc. The playing field has been levelled out for fans.

Only UK chart positions are listed and only UK singles are listed, as such. For example, 'Champagne Supernova' was never released as a single in the UK and is, therefore, not referred to as a single.

Oasis has released a lot of songs and it is very easy to access outtakes, demos, radio appearances, etc. online. Expect more 'lost tracks' to appear in the coming years, as the deluxe reissue treatment is given to their latter albums. This book will rush through the very early Oasis songs written by Liam and Bonehead, as well as the very early Noel songs that were released on various demo tapes. Because of the format of the *On Track* series, the focus is on the songs that Oasis have *officially* released at the time of this writing. Oasis have a story that is worth analysing from multiple angles, and we can hope for a comprehensive biography at some point in the future that includes cooperation from principal players.

Out Of The Blue Studios, Manchester, Autumn 1991

'Alice' (L. Gallagher, P. Arthurs)
Sometimes referred to as 'She Always Comes Up Smiling', but listed as 'Alice' on the demo tape. Noel was not terribly impressed with the song, nor was he impressed with the songwriting duo, making several jokes at their expense over the years.

'Take Me' (L. Gallagher, P. Arthurs)
One of the few pre-Noel songs that Noel has had something positive to say about, going as far as to say that he wished Liam and Bonehead would have recorded it. 'Take Me' has an interesting psychedelic vibe going on, and it may have been fun to revisit as a more fully realised band.

'Reminice' (L. Gallagher, P. Arthurs)
Sounding a bit like a discarded Stone Roses demo; not much has been said about this song since 1991.

The band quickly recognised that they needed a songwriter, with Liam recognising that Noel could potentially play some type of supporting role given his experience in the industry. Noel, calling home one day from Munich, Germany, was informed by Peggie that Liam was in a band, to which Noel responded, 'He can't fucking sing'. And so it began. With Noel back in town, he went to see Oasis perform one night and was impressed, to his surprise. Initially approached by the band to act as their manager, to which he demurred, he eventually ended up joining the band after a few jam sessions, or after begging to join if you believe Liam's telling of the tale. There is also a version of the tale which purports that Noel played Liam 'Live Forever', and Liam was so impressed that he went and advocated for Noel.

> There is the myth that I kicked open the rehearsal room door to the theme tune of *The Good, The Bad And The Ugly* and said, 'Everybody stop what they're doing, I am here to make us millionaires'. There wasn't that at all, I kind of fell into the whole thing by accident, really. I never had a clear vision of anything until Liam asked me to join and then I turned into a megalomaniac.

Noel is quick to point out that the band went nowhere for two years. A half-dozen or so demos were done with Noel in the band, among them: 'Colour My Life', 'See The Sun', 'Take Me', 'Better Let You Know', Must Be The Music' and 'Snakebyte'. The songs were slowly improving, but Noel was light years away from songs he would soon be writing and demoing for the group. Oasis started performing live more, started building up a bit of a reputation as a hot live band and Noel began writing many of the songs that would soon be defining a generation in Britain. Noel had contacted Tony Griffiths of the

Liverpool band The Real People in 1992, whom he had met while touring with the Inspiral Carpets, asking for some advice and, more importantly, if Oasis could use their studio to record some songs. In the spring of 1993, Oasis recorded around a dozen songs at their studio in Liverpool, with six of those winding up on the demo tape that is called either *Oasis Live* or, more commonly, *Live Demonstration*. The brilliance was by now almost fully formed, although The Real People would later say they wrote far more than has been formally acknowledged. In May of 1993, Oasis played their now mythical gig at King Tut's in Glasgow, where they were spotted by Alan McGee and, by the end of the night, they were signed to Creation Records. By the end of 1993, the White Label version of 'Columbia' was blowing up on the radio, and all the songs that would make up *Definitely Maybe* and the assorted B-sides had been written.

Definitely Maybe (1994)

Personnel:
Liam Gallagher: lead vocals, tambourine
Noel Gallagher: guitars, backing vocals, bass, piano, production
Paul 'Bonehead' Arthurs: rhythm guitar, piano, production
Paul 'Guigsy' McGuigan: bass guitar, production
Tony McCarroll: drums, production
Backing Vocals on 'Supersonic' by Anthony Griffiths of The Real People
Produced by Noel Gallagher & Mark Coyle
Additional production & mixing by Owen Morris
Except 'Slide Away' produced by Dave Batchelor and mixed by Owen Morris
'Supersonic' produced by Mark Coyle and mixed by Dave Scott
'Married With Children' mixed by Mark Coyle
Engineers: Anjali Dutt, Dave Scott, Roy Spong and Mark Coyle
Mastered by Owen Morris at Clear, Manchester
UK release date: 29 August 1994
Chart placings: UK: 1, US: 58

While the early 1990s saw the emergence of Blur and the release of the
seminal *Pills 'n' Thrills And Bellyaches* by Happy Mondays, the charts were
mainly dominated by dance groups and ear-candy by groups such as Take
That. The Stone Roses, whose self-titled debut became one of the most
acclaimed albums of the era, were famously taking a very long time to release
their second album, and while Suede released their debut in 1993, that album
had more in common with glam-era Bowie than with the guitars Oasis would
be associated with. As Peter Richard Adams and Matt Pooler talk about in
their excellent book *Britpop*, 1994 was the year when everything changed in
the UK, both musically and culturally. Kurt Cobain's death signalled a new
chapter in 1990s music history, notably the end of the American influence on
British alternative music. The Fred and Rosemary West murders dominated
headlines in the early part of the year and British politics were in the process
of a major overhaul, with the rising emergence of one Tony Blair. The era of
Oasis was about to begin in full force and the general public was ready for
the distraction and change of scenery.

Oasis, more so than any other band of their generation, were able to
bring people together in a way that few other artists have been able to do.
The music that Oasis created was able to speak to a generation of young
people in the UK who were tired of the direction the country had been
heading in, and who were looking for something more, or *someone* more.
A huge part of this came down to the fact that Oasis were perhaps *the* most
anthemic band of all time. Their songs resonated and continue to resonate
with fans, and their choruses are some of the most famous in history, all
creating a shared sense of experience: singing along to 'Don't Look Back In
Anger', for example. It would get to the point where every song at an Oasis

concert was an opportunity for an audience sing-along. Oasis, coming from the working-class city of Manchester, were able to resonate with fans on a deeper level than their contemporaries Blur – who came out of the art-school tradition of British rock – were arguably able to. At least part of that came down to the mass appeal that Oasis had and their ability to be seen as more authentic. Part of that authenticity had a bit of an anti-establishment tilt to it as well. Never afraid to speak their minds, swear, drink to excess or criticise institutions, the Gallagher brothers cultivated an image of being relatable, like someone you could have a pint of lager with. All of this groundwork was formally laid with *Definitely Maybe*, which is still the record that defines Oasis and their aesthetic, even if the follow-up was ultimately more popular.

The road to getting *Definitely Maybe* to completion was a relatively bumpy one, featuring multiple scraped sessions, overdubs and a fair amount of frustration. The end result is one of the most guitar-heavy, compressed and abrasive-sounding records of the era. Following their session with The Real People, which Noel felt was still the best session they had, they would record at The Pink Museum and Monnow Valley before winding up at Sawmills Studio. While at Sawmills, a variety of techniques were attempted, somewhat out of frustration, in an effort to replicate the sound they were going for. Ultimately, they figured out that one of the only ways to replicate their live sound was to record together with no barriers between them. Afterwards, Noel would then overdub guitars and sometimes other instruments. While some critics and many involved in the recording processes would criticise the end result for passing through too many hands and not sounding as intended, no one could deny the immediacy of the record, nor the sheer power of the songs. There was also the fact that the version of *Definitely Maybe*, as officially released, was one of the first to be mastered using the brick wall method, which is a recording and mastering method that maximises loudness. As such, the album was as loud as almost any other album released around the same time. If 'Supersonic' came on at the pub, it was louder than whatever song preceded it. The process of mastering *Definitely Maybe* was also a cluster, with Owen Morris being called in to try and save the day, but, depending on which perspective one takes, made everything sound worse. Morris had experience in the studio, where Mark Coyle and Noel did not have the required experience for a production of this scale. Therefore, it was hoped that a good master would fix a bad mix, even though many have since complained about what Morris ultimately came up with. Engineer Anjali Dutt, who worked with the band, would say:

> Though I don't think that the original mixes were amazing, I did prefer them to the final album, as the relentlessness of the compressed chainsaw guitars just wears you out, even if the initial feeling of excitement is invigorating...
> I think the mixes did the job and gave it that much-needed excitement and

attitude. But it wasn't my kind of sound and I found it far too abrasive, so I can only recall ever playing a few tracks at a time.

When *Definitely Maybe* was released in August 1994, Oasis came out of the door screaming in a way that only a few other artists, such as Led Zeppelin, The Stone Roses and the Sex Pistols, had ever done. Of the 11 tracks on *Definitely Maybe*, a half-dozen were cultural-defining tracks, a handful were just damn good and maybe one or two were just 'okay'. Other contemporaries like Blur, Pulp and even Radiohead would not arrive nearly as fully formed as Oasis had. Their second record would have bigger hits, but in the eyes of many, they never bettered what they did on *Definitely Maybe*. It was the perfect moment in the decade for an album like this to be released, it was the perfect distillation of Noel's songwriting and the perfect execution of Liam's perfect sneering vocals. While they would be more famous in 1995 and beyond, 1994 is, in many ways, the most important year in the career of Oasis. 1994 starts with the band getting a boost in public love and support from their 'Columbia' demo; it ends with Oasis as one of the most popular bands in the UK, with a number of critically acclaimed singles behind them, including some tremendous B-sides that often eclipse some of the A-sides. In between, there was *Top Of The Pops*, the cover of the *NME*, a famous John Harris interview, etc. Starting with the release of *Definitely Maybe* and through their performance at Knebworth in 1996, Oasis were the biggest band in Britain – these are the tunes that started it.

'Rock 'n' Roll Star' (N. Gallagher)

For many people, especially in America, where the early singles were not as easy to find, this was their first exposure to Oasis. As far as opening clarion calls go, it does not get much better than this. 'Rock 'n' Roll Star' plays the exact same role in Oasis mythology as 'I Wanna Be Adored' plays in Stone Roses mythology or 'Welcome To The Jungle' for Guns N' Roses. It is their statement of purpose, their call to arms. A classically Oasis-esque blend of soaring melodies and guitars with some psychedelia tossed in at the end for good measure, 'Rock 'n' Roll Star' spends a little over five minutes showing listeners a lot of the musical tricks that would define their sound, while lyrically, it is perhaps their ultimate escape song. As Alex Niven explains in his book on *Definitely Maybe* from the 33 1/3 book series:

In 'Rock 'n' Roll Star', Noel Gallagher's alternative plan was to get a car and drive it as far as he could away from Manchester, a plan that was ambitious given that he had no money and had never learned how to drive... Gallagher's argument went something like this: you tell us to become wealthy, then, with a ridiculous leap of imagination, we'll pretend we're the wealthiest people in the world; you tell us to get on our bikes and look for work, we'll get in a car and discover our dreams; you tell us to aim high, we'll reach for the heavens. Many of the songs from the *Definitely Maybe* era, both singles, albums and B-sides, were about leaving or about going somewhere or reaching for something new.

While Noel wrote the song, of course, this is Liam's song: always has been and continues to be. Many of his solo shows still open with 'Rock 'n' Roll Star', and he recently gave a great rendition of the tune at the One Love Manchester show in 2017. While Liam is justifiably considered an all-time great frontman, his trademark snarl eventually became something journalists and casual fans would make fun of. Here, though, throughout the entire song, Liam masterfully delivers every one of Noel's words as if he had been singing this song for years. When he delivers the masterful hook 56 seconds into the song, starting with 'I live my life for the stars that shine', it's hard not to sing along and get excited. An underrated aspect of this song is the background vocals that Noel masterfully provides and would continue to do so throughout Oasis' career.

The first verse is sung twice, the soaring chorus hits the listener twice and four minutes have passed, with some listeners maybe feeling like they are rock and roll stars. At about 4:28, Liam reminds the listener, 'it's just rock 'n' roll', going on to repeat the mantra eight times. As if waking up from a dream that the previous four and a half minutes encapsulated: escape, freedom and opportunity, just rock and roll clichés and dreams. Yet, the next few years would find Oasis scaling heights that even 'Rock 'n' Roll Star' could not have predicted. Noel Gallagher would say that 'Rock 'n' Roll Star' was the whole manifesto of Oasis wrapped up in one song, and while he was known to change his mind a lot when asked this same question, he told *Q Magazine* in 2008 that this was his favourite Oasis track:

The words and the sentiment of that song, that's what it's all about. I remember bringing it down to the lads in the rehearsal studio and rehearsing it until the first time we played it live. There was a hush after it, and it wasn't the hush of people going, 'What was that all about?' It was silenced awe. No one had ever said it in a song before. Tonight, I'm a rock 'n' roll star.

'Rock 'n' Roll Star' was released as a single in America in 1995, but never in the UK. Also appearing on the best-of compilation *Stop The Clocks* and the *Familiar To Millions* live album, it would be tough to make a list of essential Oasis songs and leave this tune off. A staple of almost every single Oasis tour, as well as Liam's solo shows, it doesn't get much better than this until about track three.

'Shakermaker' (N. Gallagher)
A-side single. Released: 20 June 1994. UK: 11
The second *Definitely Maybe* single and, as of 2021, the only single from the band's first two albums not to reach at least platinum status in the UK. A

slightly odd choice for release as a single, especially when 'Slide Away' and 'Rock 'n' Roll Star' were available for single release. Released two months before *Definitely Maybe* and two months after 'Supersonic', it continued to build excitement for Oasis throughout the UK. It moves through a slinky, 12-bar blues progression that Noel says was inspired, even borrowed, from the obscure Beatles instrumental 'Flying'. Listening back to that *Magical Mystery Tour* cut, it's tough to hear much of a similarity, save for maybe the slow-moving pace of the music. If you tried really hard and imagined replacing Lennon's Mellotron with a guitar, you may get a 'Shakermaker' vibe and perhaps that's what Noel meant when he cited the song as inspiration. Noel has always been a master of composing a solid bridge and 'Shakermaker' is no exception, with the middle-eight coming in at 2:21, giving the song a needed catchy break before returning to the slinky melody.

This is the least exciting of the four singles released from *Definitely Maybe*, and one could easily argue that more deserving singles could have been released from the debut. 'Shakermaker' is still an enjoyable song thanks in large part to Noel's nonsensical lyrics, with mentions of Mr. Ben, Mr. Clean and Mister Sifter. Noel likely loved the excuse to use Mr. Clean in a song, as it is also the title of a song by one of Noel's favourite bands: The Jam. Yet, within the lyrics exists that same yearning to escape, to break out of the England that Thatcher had created. The first line states, 'I'd like to be somebody else and not know where I've been', and it's hard to picture Noel writing that and not imagining a future somewhere better or different. Lacking a final verse, Noel quickly wrote one in the back of a taxi while heading to record the song.

There would be several notable instances in the early career of Oasis where Noel would be accused of stealing a line, a riff or a melody. 'Shakermaker' was one such instance and, eventually, the songwriting credit was adjusted to reflect his using the melody from 'I'd Like To Teach The World To Sing (In Perfect Harmony)' written by Roger Cook, Roger Greenway, Bill Backer and Billy Davis. Listening to the song, there is an uncanny resemblance to 'Shakemaker'. The Oasis tribute band No Way Sis released a cover of 'I'd Like To Teach The World To Sing' but styled as 'Shakermaker'. More famously, the original melody was used in the ad campaign for Coca-Cola, I'd Like to Buy the World a Coke. 'Shakermaker' was played live consistently through 1996, when it was more or less dropped for the rest of their career, save for a resurgence in 2000.

'Live Forever' (N. Gallagher)
A-side single. Released: 8 August 1994. UK: 10
The tune that changed everything, both for Oasis and for British music, not to mention its huge cultural impact. A moment of silence, a soft-spoken 'oh yea' and a standard drum beat give way to perhaps the single greatest sound to Oasis fans: Liam's perfect delivery of 'maybeee' to kick off what some will

say is the greatest Oasis song of them all. For a lot of Oasis fans in the UK, in August 1994, when the 'Live Forever' single was released, there was a sense that this was a generation-defining tune. Released about three weeks before *Definitely Maybe*, it gave the record-buying public a strong idea of what they were going to get with the full album.

Noel presented a fully formed version of 'Live Forever' to the band in early 1993, after starting work on the song in 1991. According to Tony McCarroll, and as one could imagine, the band was floored by what they heard. When Creation boss Alan McGee recalled the first time he heard the song, he simply said, 'it was probably the single greatest moment I've ever experienced with them'. For all the praise that the song would garner, both immediately and over subsequent decades, it's a shockingly simple song based on just a few chords and no real chorus. As others have pointed out, including Bonehead, this simplicity meant the song never really resolved; it would keep going. On a practical level, this meant that, when played live, the song could end at different points and in different ways. On a spiritual level, however, this gave the song even more power. It could belong to anybody at any time. Fans and critics have garnered different meanings from the lyrics over the years. Some interpret the song as a tribute to Noel's mother, Peggie. Others interpret the song to be about a relationship, perhaps a friendship. Noel would say of the track:

> It's a song about having a friend who could be your friend for life. The lyrics go, 'Maybe I don't really want to know/How your garden grows', and I think that's just saying, 'I don't care about your bad points, I love you for the good in you'. I knew when I wrote it that this album was going to be the most important album of its era.

In recent years, Noel has spoken of his effusive love for Nirvana and Kurt Cobain in particular. Part of the origin story of 'Live Forever' involves Cobain and what was, at the time, a relatively obscure Nirvana song. Noel has mentioned several times over the years that he heard the Nirvana song 'I Hate Myself And Want To Die' and he felt it was totally rubbish and set out to write a song that was the total opposite, hence, 'Live Forever'. Noel would elaborate:

> That cunt is sitting in his mansion in Seattle, on smack, he's got everything, he's got the world at his feet, right, he's in the biggest and most revered band in the world today, and he fucking hates himself and he fucking wants to die. I was like: 'I'm not fucking 'aving that! Bollocks! He might have been depressed, but there's no need to bring everybody else down!'

Several aspects of this story don't totally hold up to scrutiny, however. The song 'I Hate Myself And Want To Die' was first recorded as a demo in early

1993, and the second and final recording was done in February 1993. It was not included on *In Utero,* which was released in September 1993, but was instead released as the opening track on *The Beavis and Butt-Head Experience* soundtrack, released in November 1993. By late 1993, when Noel *could* have heard the song for the first time, 'Live Forever' had long been written, demoed and was in their setlist. More likely, what happened was that Noel wrote the song, recorded it and it served as a contrast to the Nirvana track, providing some nice, little soundbites. Nirvana aside, Noel credits The Rolling Stones for helping him with the melody, especially the song 'Shine A Light' from *Exile On Main Street* and the bit of the song where Mick sings 'May the god lord shine a light on you'.

Released as a single in August 1994, the cover of the single is a black and white photo of John Lennon's childhood home, one of many direct references to The Beatles, and Lennon in particular, throughout the band's career. Were they suggesting that Lennon would live forever, or confirming he already was? The more famous of the two music videos made for 'Live Forever' features the band in New York's Central Park, specifically the Strawberry Fields Memorial. Famously, it also included Liam sitting on a chair that was affixed to a wall, seemingly just floating in the air. The second version of the video, geared towards the American audience, shows the band in an office with pictures of famous rock stars who had passed away, including the recent addition of Kurt Cobain.

Upon release, 'Live Forever' made critics take note of Oasis. 'Supersonic' and 'Shakermaker' were good tunes, but 'Live Forever' stopped people in their tracks. While only peaking at number ten on the charts, its popularity and acclaim have only grown in recent years. Fans can rank the songs how they like, but this one always appears towards or at the top of the mountain. Several publications have ranked it as the greatest song ever written, and as recently as 2023, took the top spot on the Radio X annual poll of the Best British Song of All Time. An obvious crowd favourite at concerts, second only to maybe 'Don't Look Back In Anger', 'Live Forever' was played at the majority of Oasis concerts. A few times, the crowd alone would sing the song from start to finish. There are plenty of famous versions of the song, and in recent years, it served as a tribute to the victims of the Manchester Arena Attack as well as a tribute to Taylor Hawkins in 2022. Released on *Familiar To Millions, Stop The Clocks* and *Time Flies...1994-2009,* 'Live Forever' is perhaps the definitive Oasis track, with a melody and hook that are tough to beat and lyrics that can resonate with anyone. Regarding the song itself, is it an intimate love song? An anthem? A little of both? The song is whatever it needs to be to whoever is listening to it. We see things they'll never see, after all.

'Up In The Sky' (N. Gallagher)
This features a riff that perhaps sounds like an untrained musician trying to play 'Day Tripper' on an out-of-tune guitar with distortion. This is not to say

by any means that Noel is untrained, but simply to point out that the track bears some resemblance to The Beatles of the mid-1960s. One of a few songs on the first two albums that perhaps goes 'under the radar', this track sees Noel questioning the establishment figures in and around Britain: '...Tell me how high do you think you'll go before you start falling', with Liam's sneer adding a punch to the question of 'how does it feel' and the statement of 'welcome to my world'. A great pop hook comes in at 1:47 with 'you'll need assistance with the things that you have never ever seen': Noel's insistence that the politicians, who act as if they are up in the sky, are incredibly out of touch with the common people in Britain, of whom Noel was brethren with when writing these early songs – a very common man himself. These similar themes were also being explored by Blur and Pulp around this time, arguably to greater effect.

The demo sounds remarkably similar to the version that would end up on *Definitely Maybe*, just a little more rough around the edges. An acoustic version would be released as a B-side on the 'Live Forever' single. While perhaps the least-favourite song on side A of the album, the song serves its purpose as something of a reset between the highs of 'Live Forever' and the swirling 'Columbia'.

'Columbia' (N. Gallagher)

For some, this is a fan favourite and one of the great Oasis tracks, while for others, it is too long and less effective than the demo version. Either way, this glorious display of swirling guitars and psychedelic undertones is one of the most popular Oasis album tracks. In many ways, 'Columbia' was the first Oasis song that the general public heard, the demo version being released to radio stations in late 1993. It's a little shoegaze, a little Madchester and a little 1960s rock. One of the most densely layered Oasis songs of the era, much of the credit belongs to Owen Morris, for better or for worse.

When track five hits on *Definitely Maybe,* we get a couple of seconds of silence, leading into the faint sounds of distorted guitars rising in volume and Tony McCarroll hitting his drumsticks together to provide the beat. It's a swirling mess of guitars, in the best way, until Liam starts singing at about 1:08:

There we were now here we are
All this confusion nothing's the same to me

The opening couplet has led many fans to speculate, or rather hope, that if and when an Oasis reunion happened, they would open with this song. Arguably more so than any other song on *Definitely Maybe*, there is controversy over the lyrical authorship: are they Noel's lyrics, or did Chris Griffiths of The Real People write them? Regarding that controversy and the genesis of the song, Noel says:

When we started, we didn't have a lot of songs, so we would jam out current Acid House favourites and fuck about. 'Columbia' derived from one of those nights. It was an instrumental and we played it the first night I ever did a gig with Oasis. When we started at The Real People's studio, somebody had the idea of adding lyrics and it's still a bone of contention to this day who actually wrote the words. We were all on acid at the time, but I know I wrote 90% of them.

A song in which the music matters more than the lyrics, it makes sense that it started as an instrumental jam. Bonehead's favourite song to play live, 'Columbia' was a mainstay of the setlist throughout the *Heathen Chemistry Tour*. Most famously, they opened up their canonical Knebworth 1996 show with 'Columbia'; Liam interacted with fans and gave off nothing but good vibes as he waited for his cue to jump in. Chris Griffiths, who was at that very show, probably felt none of those good vibes, realising that he would never be properly credited – at least as he should be, in his mind.

'Supersonic' (N. Gallagher)
A-side single. Released: 11 April 1994. UK: 31

The first single from one of the greatest singles bands of all time. In the words of Noel Gallagher, 'we hit the ground runnin' with that one', and it's hard to argue against him. Written and recorded in one night in Liverpool, this is the song that Noel said separated Oasis from the other bands at the time who, in Noel's mind, were trying to be a little too clever with their lyrics and themes. With 'Supersonic', Noel had written a set of admittedly nonsensical, yet hilarious lyrics that do not demand to be taken seriously. These are backed by an incredibly catchy melody and a hook to die for in "Cause my friend said he'd take you home'.

The rhyming of the lyrics is perhaps the most famous part of the song, sometimes referred to as doggerel rhymes as they are irregular and done for comic effect: 'I'm feeling supersonic/Give me gin and tonic', 'I know a girl called Elsa/She's into Alka-Seltzer', 'She done it with a doctor, on a helicopter'. Played in the key of A major, musically, the song is dominated by power chords and features one of Noel's most famous arpeggiated guitar riffs. The very first lines of the song, however, are anything but silly: 'I need to be myself/I can't be no one else'. These are the words that Liam chose when asked about his favourite Oasis lyric.

The band had gone into the studio hoping to get a good take of 'Bring It On Down' for release as their first single, but to no avail. A frustrated Noel retreated to a back room where, in his own words, he wrote 'Supersonic' in about a half hour, finding inspiration in a jam that the band was playing. Special inspiration was surely taken from Tony McCarroll's steady beat, apparently causing Noel to tell him to 'keep that going', while Noel ironed out the entire song. Noel did a guide vocal for Liam, who proceeded to nail the song with one take. Whether Noel had it up his sleeve, lying in wait, or it truly came together from start to finish that evening, the song was finished and recorded within 11 hours at Pink Museum Studio in Liverpool. 'Take Me Away' was also recorded this same evening. Over the years, a little more nuance has been given to the story, as would often happen given Noel's knack for embellishing and changing stories around. The net result is a general consensus that Tony, Bonehead and Guigsy deserve some credit for composing the song. Tony Griffiths also provided background vocals on the track and even Liam has chimed in, saying he wrote some of the lyrics.

Containing one of the great hooks in the Oasis canon and some terrific Noel playing, both in the intro and his rather spiralling solo at the end of the song, 'Supersonic' has established itself as one of the defining songs of the Britpop era. Not as universally appealing as 'Live Forever' or 'Slide Away', 'Supersonic' has, nonetheless, become a signature song and has been played at a majority of Oasis concerts since 1994, with a slight pause during the *Heathen Chemistry Tour* era. It also frequently appears at Liam shows and Noel has even been known to bust it out from time to time. Released on both *Stop The Clocks* and *Time Flies...1994-2009* as well as on *Familiar To Millions*, this was an incredible way to launch what would be an incredible career. A straw poll of fan-favourite Oasis songs would squarely place this song towards the top.

The cover for the 'Supersonic' single, designed by Mircodot, featured a terrific colour scheme that would not have looked out of place in a Michael Mann movie. The rest of the band almost look like wax figurines behind Liam, who is dressed in blue and looking cool as ever with his leather jacket. Oasis made their UK television debut on 18 March 1994 when they performed 'Supersonic' on the Channel 4 show *The Word*. Bonehead would recall that there were a lot of nerves, given that the band were not miming but playing for real. A major concern, at least for Bonehead, was what shirt to wear. Upon hitting that first note of 'Supersonic', however, all was well. And all would be well, at least for a little while. A magical song indeed.

'Bring It On Down' (N. Gallagher)

Perhaps the most punk-sounding song in the Oasis canon, this tune is a tribute to The Stooges, the MC5 and punk rock, in the words of Noel. It also features some distorted vocals from Liam during the second verse, which would be unusual for an Oasis song. The lyrics even have a rare Oasis punk edge:

You're the outcast, you're the underclass
But you don't care, because you're living fast

Like 'Up In The Sky' or 'Cigarettes & Alcohol', there is a political undercurrent here. Alan McGee, apparently obsessing over the above lyrics, excitedly insisted it should be the first single. Perhaps due to fate, they weren't able to get a good take and they wound up with 'Supersonic' instead, a far better choice for a single. Reflecting on the lyrics and the political implications, Noel would remark;

> I don't sit down and think politics: let's get to the bones of this shit. But at that point, I was unemployed, in rented accommodation, trying to make it in the world, living from one week to the next, not knowing if you're gonna have enough money for a pizza. You are in a political situation even if you don't realise it …

Setting the scene with their best punk imitation, the song begins with distortion and the sound of drumsticks clicking, before drummer Tony McCarroll starts pounding the drums. McCarroll does not get a lot of love for being the drummer in Oasis and is likely most famous for being fired. This is not to downplay his role in the early Oasis sound, but he was constantly put down by Noel and would later sue the band, which did not endear him to certain Oasis fans. Producer Owen Morris would say when describing McCarroll: 'Tony was quiet and always polite to me but seemed out of his depth… so I think Tony did well to survive as long as he did in Oasis'. He would also describe McCarroll's drumming style as 'extremely basic' but with perfect timing and tempo. He was the right drummer for *Definitely Maybe,* but Noel would famously say that 'he wouldn't have been able to drum the new songs' when they were about to record their second album. Tony would publish an autobiography titled *Oasis: The Truth,* which includes a chapter called 'Arise Sir Noel, The Lord Mayor Of Loneliness'. The book clearly seeks to settle a few scores, but it's an enjoyable and fun read if the reader takes it with a grain or two of salt.

'Cigarettes & Alcohol' (N. Gallagher)
A-side single. Released: 10 October 1994. UK: 7
Excitement for new Oasis material was such that at the time of this single release, *Definitely Maybe* had already been out for nearly a month and a half, three singles had already been released, and this, the fourth single from *Definitely Maybe*, climbed to number seven on the UK charts. More so than any other Oasis single/EP release up to this point, the 'Cigarettes & Alcohol' release contained three other songs that were all worth the price of admission, making this their best single up to this point and one of their best ever. 'Cigarettes & Alcohol' remains one of the great rock songs from *Definitely Maybe*, a party anthem with some of Noel's best lines and Liam's brilliant delivery. It also serves as the second song from *Definitely Maybe* that would see Oasis accused of plagiarism. Noel would recall when he first presented the song to Bonehead in the rehearsal room:

…And it started up with the riff and the guitar, and he was going, 'Woah, woah, woah, woah, woah, you can't fucking do that, that's fucking T-Rex!' I said, 'I don't give a fuck, it's fucking Oasis now!' I remember the first time that Liam sang it, and it was one of the first times I thought, 'fuck me, he's got a good voice…'

The opening riff is unmistakably 'Get It On' by T-Rex; when Liam starts singing, it is unmistakably Oasis, wondering aloud if he has finally found something worth living for in the titular cigarettes and alcohol. The song contains some of Noel's most (in)famous lyrics: 'you might as well do the white line' and, of course, 'is it worth the aggravation to find yourself a job when there's nothing worth working for?' This attitude that Noel and the rest of the band possessed, one of not caring and being brutally honest, was very refreshing in the eyes of journalist Paolo Hewitt, who wrote one of the great Oasis books documenting their peak years. Regarding 'Cigarettes & Alcohol', Paolo relays that the band knew they would get sued for the T-Rex similarities and didn't care. 'Cigarettes & Alcohol' also played directly into the theme running through *Definitely Maybe*, which Noel would say was 'Let's have it'.

> …All the songs were about leaving Manchester and ending up in the sunshine, taking drugs and drinking for the rest of your life… it's all about escapism – a pint in one hand, your best mate in the other and just having a good time.

A concert warhorse, 'Cigarettes & Alcohol' was a part of every Oasis tour, and while lacking the universal anthemic quality of 'Live Forever', it has become one of their most famous songs. Perhaps most interestingly of all, the song was covered by Rod Stewart for his 1998 album *When We Were the New Boys* and is featured as the opening track. The less said about this cover version, the better. This song was meant to be sung by one man and one man alone: Liam Gallagher.

'Digsy's Dinner' (N. Gallagher)
An easy target for the least essential song from *Definitely Maybe*, this quirky song still has its charms. Lyrically, It's silly and ridiculous, but that is the point, of course:

> What a life it would be
> If you could come to mine for tea
> I'll pick you up at half past three
> We'll have lasagna

The band had a friend named Digsy, who was in the studio one day joking about lasagna while Noel was apparently messing about on drums. Alan

McGee would say that he felt the song was a parody of Oasis' Britpop rivals Blur – there is, after all, an unmistakable Blur vibe going on. More importantly, 'Digsy's Dinner' is a song that could only have appeared on *Definitely Maybe*. Noel would comment on the song;

> If you wrote 'Digsy's Dinner' now, *The Guardian* or the music papers would destroy you. It's a song about going to someone's house for lasagna – you only write songs like that when you're free of inhibitions.

'Slide Away' (Gallagher)
This glorious number features what Noel would refer to as Liam's best-ever vocal effort. It is a beloved song; for many, it is *the* definitive Oasis statement. When Tom Howards ranked every Oasis song in order of greatness for the *NME* in 2019, this song appeared in the very top spot. Because of this effusive praise, there is also a contingent of Oasis fans who refer to this as one of the more overrated of their songs. For this author, it is properly rated as a masterpiece, if perhaps not their definitive masterpiece.

Written on the Les Paul he had been gifted from Johnny Marr of The Smiths, this represents one of the major leaps in Noel's songwriting. 'Slide Away' also contains perhaps the archetypal *soaring* Noel melody, which he was just beginning to hone. In hindsight, this is a song that should have been released as a single, with Noel apparently stopping the label from doing as much with the claim that five singles from a debut would be too many. Most fans would likely agree that 'Slide Away' is only second to 'Live Forever' on the debut, perhaps the best pure album track they ever released. This love song was quickly knocked out in the studio, and according to Noel, the song wrote itself. Inspired again by Noel's girlfriend at the time, Louise Jones, the song was written about their rollercoaster of a relationship: 'I dream of you and we talk of growing old, but you said please don't'. The ending coda, where Noel sings, 'Don't know, don't care, all I know is you can take me there', is truly one of the great moments in the Oasis songbook. As the only song that made it out alive from the aborted Dave Batchelor Monnow Valley sessions, it has a marked difference in how it sounds in contrast with other songs on the album. The end result is a much more polished, or produced sound, than any other song on *Definitely Maybe*.

The guitar work would not sound out of place on a Crazy Horse record, with some arguing that Noel modelled 'Slide Away' on the melody to Neil Young's 'Hey, Hey, My, My (Into The Black)'. The A minor 7th chord, which was so prevalent on many of Neil Young's greatest epics, is the centrepiece here. Noel Gallagher allegedly once described the song as trying to combine The Smiths' 'Reel Around The Fountain' with Neil Young, which is an odd but perhaps apt description. Equally influential, perhaps, was The Verve and their guitarist Nick McCabe. Oasis toured with The Verve prior to the release of *Definitely Maybe* and they would remain close with the band, especially leader and vocalist Richard Ashcroft, whom Noel would write 'Cast No Shadow' for. The Verve's debut full-length album was released in 1993, titled *A Storm in Heaven*. The guitar-drenched album certainly would have been an influence on Noel Gallagher's writing. The most popular song on the album was a brilliant track called 'Slide Away', perhaps a direct influence on the relatively similar-sounding penultimate track on *Definitely Maybe*.

Both Gallagher brothers would lament that the song was not performed even more in concert than it already was, each of them recognising its power. It was played frequently but was not played at every show. Check out the Knebworth 1996 version for a truly stellar performance. Noel claims that Liam feels the song drags on a bit at the end and that's why they removed it from many of their latter-era setlists, even though it was a standard song on the *Dig Out Your Soul Tour*. Liam, especially, has continued to perform the song live and Noel notably performed the song in 2007, which was then released on the solo album *The Dreams We Have As Children*. Ask most Oasis fans to rank their top five Oasis tracks and this one is almost always on that list. *NME* ranked it as the 57th greatest Britpop song ever, and then in 2019, *NME* ranked it as the greatest Oasis song ever, as previously stated. Paul McCartney also claims this to be his favourite Oasis song, which surely must bring Noel immense joy. It would, however, be too easy to end a masterful album with a song this perfect.

'Married With Children' (N. Gallagher)
While it would have been easy, and perhaps it would have even made sense, to end the album with 'Slide Away', 'Married With Children' is a needed track. Another moment of levity, this one features a terrifically self-aware set of lyrics, and some of Noel's most basic, yet effortlessly efficient acoustic guitar work. It was written in producer Owen Coyle's bedroom, allegedly on John Squire's acoustic guitar, which happened to be at Coyle's house.

Lyrically, the song was again inspired by Noel's then-girlfriend Louise Jones, who has several claims to fame in Oasis lore. This song, as well as 'Slide Away', was inspired by her and perhaps more notably, she was the first person to ever hear 'Live Forever', although Noel has said she was unimpressed. Noel would tell *Melody Maker* that he saw an episode of the American sitcom *Married...With Children* and 'I looked at them two in the show, and looked at us two, and I thought, that's us! That is!' Noel wanted anyone to be able to relate to the lyrics, as they list things that a couple would hate about each other.

I hate the way that even though you know you're wrong
You say you're right
I hate the books you read and all your friends
Your music's shite, it keeps me up all night, all night

The song is short and sweet and provides an opportunity for a comedown after the soaring heights of 'Slide Away'. A part of some concert setlists in 1994 and 1995, this song would fall out of rotation, with a very brief resurgence on the *Heathen Chemistry Tour*, which was just as well. As the crowds got bigger and rowdier, this would be a tough song to justify in a live setting. It is the perfect low-key ending to a very high-energy album.

Definitely Maybe B-Sides/EPs

If nothing else is true about Oasis, they were an amazing singles band. In the grand tradition of The Beatles, The Jam, The Smiths or Blur, Oasis would release singles that essentially functioned as EPs, full of amazing B-sides that were often better than the A-sides. When The Beatles or The Jam would release a single, it would include at least two songs: one A-side and one B-side. All of the classic-era Oasis singles would include the A-side and three B sides, and in fact, it was not until the release of 'Go Let It Out' in 2000 that any Oasis single had less than four songs. This would mean that every time Oasis released a single, fans were able to hear three songs that were not included on any other album. Between 1994 and 1998, Oasis would release 12 UK singles, meaning there were 36 B-sides amongst those singles that were not included on any of the first three albums. Oasis would continue to release singles throughout their career, but the ones between 1994 and 1998 are typically considered the most consistent, especially 1994-1996. Many of these B-sides are considered some of the best Oasis songs ever: 'The Masterplan', 'Talk Tonight', 'Round Are Way', 'Acquiesce', etc.

'Sad Song' (N. Gallagher)

Not a B-side per se, but only included on the UK vinyl release and Japanese CD version of *Definitely Maybe*, this is an essential track from the era, awash in Am7 chords and with a set of Noel's best early lyrics. It is a song about the woes in life and can also be read as a conversation between two people in a dead-end town, again touching on the feeling of maybe dreaming of getting out but being resigned to a stasis.

> Where we're living in this town
> The sun is coming up and it's going down
> But it's all just the same at the end of the day
> And we cheat and we lie
> Nobody says it's wrong
> So we don't ask why
> Cause it's all just the same at the end of the day

Noel would refer to this song as a hidden gem and he is absolutely spot on. This song would not have necessarily worked on *Definitely Maybe*, but it is exquisite. It was performed a dozen or so times in 1994 and once in 1995, before being dropped from setlists. In later years as solo artists, both Noel and Liam have played the song. While Noel performs faithful renditions of the original recording, it is a song that Liam absolutely makes his own and plenty of terrific versions float around with Liam on lead vocals, including one featured in the 2016 *Oasis: Supersonic* film.

'Take Me Away' (N. Gallagher)
B-side of 'Supersonic'

Tellingly, the first Oasis B-side is a song where Noel sings lead vocals. Even though 'Sad Song' was not a B-side, it was indicative of a formula that would be followed for almost the entirety of their career. The A-side would be a popular album track 'with a couple of exceptions', almost always sung by Liam, and then on the B-sides, Noel and Liam would essentially split vocals, with Noel doing more of the slower numbers. Noel took some time to find his footing and gain confidence as a singer. Where Liam, as frontman and lead vocalist, would occupy the majority of vocals on the albums over the course of their career, sharing vocals on B-sides allowed Noel to record numerous low-key ballads such as this one, which would have been the second song that any Oasis fan would have heard given 'Supersonic' was their first official single released months before *Definitely Maybe*.

Several interpretations of the lyrics exist, from Noel's desire to escape to a commentary on his relationship with Liam:

I could be you if I wanted to, but I've never got the time
You could be me, and pretty soon you will be

It was recorded in December 1993 at Pink Museum Studios in Liverpool at the same session that would ultimately yield 'Supersonic'. Recording engineer Dave Scott recalls the song:

Was recorded in about a half hour, Noel on his own and in one take, no probs. We overdubbed the slide guitar, which was an Epiphone acoustic played with a half-pint glass, I seem to remember. Coyle put it through an old Roland Space Echo and then I mixed it in 5 minutes.

Noel's vocals aren't as assured as they would be on future songs, even on their next single release. However, the melody here is very pleasing and what we are left with is a pleasant, if oft-forgotten, early ballad from Noel.

'I Will Believe (Live)' (N. Gallagher)
B-side of 'Supersonic'

The first three Oasis single releases would follow a relatively similar pattern. The A-side single itself, followed by an acoustic track, all performed by Noel in this case, followed by a demo-esque version of a song, then finally, a live or demo version of a future album track 'at the time of release'. By the time Oasis released their fourth single, 'Cigarettes & Alcohol', Oasis entered something of a Purple Period where every EP/single would include B-sides that were often equal to or even better than the A-side counterparts. As such, the 'Supersonic', 'Shakermaker' and 'Live Forever' releases contain some of the only forgotten tracks from the early Oasis years. For proof, look no further than *The Masterplan*, released in November of 1998 by Creation Records, which collects the best Oasis B-sides and fan favourites: no B-sides from the first three Oasis singles are included. This effectively means that, especially for American Oasis fans, many people never heard these B-sides. 'I Will Believe (Live)' is a song that certainly fits into this forgotten category.

This was recorded at Pink Museum Studios in Liverpool in December 1993 at the same session where they intended to record 'Bring It On Down' for single release, but wound up with a complete version of 'Supersonic' instead. Dave Scott recalls working on this song and trying to get a decent take when the energy started falling to an all-time low; they switched gears and Noel quickly pounded out the version of 'Take Me Away' that appears on 'Supersonic'. Scott would also derisively refer to 'I Will Believe' as 'shoe-gazer shit', saying he knew they were capable of much more.

It opens with slightly distorted chiming guitars, before being joined by bass and drums, creating a pleasant melody line. The song feels like a rough demo but is certainly one of the catchier songs Noel wrote during this era. The chorus, especially, is one that, with a little polish, could have been an album track and is an incredible little earworm.

'Columbia (White Label Demo)' (N. Gallagher)
B-side of 'Supersonic'
Where the *Definitely Maybe* version of 'Columbia' is a psychedelic gem of a song awash in swirling guitars, the so-called white label demo is a much more piercing version of the song – the guitars almost sound as if they could cut someone. This version does retain some of the grooviness of the album track and remains essential to the band's legacy and the growth of their legend.

Alan McGee, founder of Creation Records, would cite 'Columbia', presented to him on a demo tape, as the track that really got him into the band, equating the song to having a Happy Mondays vibe. It is easy to imagine 'Columbia' being performed by Happy Mondays, as the song does possess that baggy, Madchester vibe that Noel had certainly been paying attention to. Pete Mitchell, Manchester-born broadcaster, would cite the constant playing of 'Columbia' by Radio One as a sign that they were making it outside of Manchester. Regarding this version of 'Columbia' getting airtime, Richard Bowes writes:

> This kind of exposure for an unknown band was unheard of and everyone within the Oasis camp, specifically those at Creation Records, was jubilant.

Alan McGee claims that to be the moment in which he knew they were going to be massive.

Simon Mason, a close associate of the band, has said: 'That white label of 'Columbia' is, to this day and always will be, one of the most remarkable pieces of music ever'.

'D'Yer Wanna Be A Spaceman?' (N. Gallagher)
B-side of 'Shakermaker'

This was the first B-side on their second single and already an improvement on the acoustic Noel track from their first single, 'Take Me Away'. This is not to say that it was a bad song, but 'D'Yer Wanna Be a Spaceman?' presents listeners with a much more assured and confident Noel. A dreamy song opening with a lightly strummed guitar, the song puts Noel's vocals at the forefront. A charming and catchy melody with lyrics, not dissimilar to 'Fade Away', that speaks of growing up and losing sight of our dreams and childhood memories, the song has been a mainstay of Noel Gallagher shows, intermittently at least, since it was written.

A rare instance of Liam providing backing vocals for Noel, it would have been hard to find a place for this on *Definitely Maybe,* so this really is a B-side in the truest sense of the word. Any flaws in the production or lyrics are neutralised by the nearly effortless way in which Noel delivers this song. Legend has it that this song was originally demoed at Mark Coyle's house in Manchester and, lyrically, it fits squarely with other songs that Noel was writing at the time, which dealt with a yearning to escape. Look no further than 'Rock 'n' Roll Star', 'Take Me Away' or 'Shakermaker'.

> It's funny how your dreams change as you're growing old
> You don't wanna be no spaceman, you just want gold
> All the dream stealers are lying in wait
> But if you wanna be a spaceman it's still not too late

The changing of the spelling in the song title would be an early example of Oasis taking a page out of Suede's playbook. Oddly enough, this has been a song that Liam has covered in this post-Oasis oeuvre, despite being strongly associated with Noel – and perhaps that is exactly why he plays it.

'Alive (8 Track Demo)' (N. Gallagher)
B-side of 'Shakermaker'

It's a shame they never gave this track the attention it deserves by properly recording and mastering it. Sounding not unlike 'Everlong' by The Foo Fighters at times, this is a song that really could have been a hit, and, again, a song lesser bands would kill for. In the 2014 *Definitely Maybe* reissue liner notes, Noel would confirm this sentiment:

I was writing songs so fast at the time, I'd write about four a week ... 'Alive' was one of the ones that never really made it but had a great vibe to it. We were progressing so fast that it was difficult for the catalogue that we had to keep up. Things were just getting binned all the time.

Noel was writing songs so quickly, a majority of which were pretty damn good. As such, a song like 'Alive', which had plenty of potential, is hidden as a B-side and never really finished.

'Bring It On Down (Live)' (N. Gallagher)
B-side of 'Shakermaker'
'Good Evening Great Britain – Hello!' Liam introduces the band with these words as Tony lays down the pounding drum intro to this great rocker. It's fun to hear a live version and it is a rocking one but does not match the production and instrumentation of the *Definitely Maybe* version.

'Up In The Sky (Acoustic)' (N. Gallagher)
B-side to 'Live Forever'
'Live Forever' was the third single released by Oasis, coming out in August 1994, still a month before *Definitely Maybe* would hit shelves. There is a little irony in the fact that this, perhaps their strongest song ever, is accompanied by three of their weakest B-sides. The first three Oasis singles all featured an alternate or a live version of a song that would also appear on *Definitely Maybe*. In the instance of this version of 'Up In The Sky', however, it is so dissimilar as to almost feel like a different song completely, this one being acoustic and sung by Noel, complete with *Led Zeppelin III*-esque psychedelic acoustic guitar sounds. Noel offers a much more restrained vocal delivery than Liam in this case. Up until the point that Noel begins singing, it is hard to tell that this is the same 'Up In The Sky' that appeared on the LP. The guitar intro here is clean, subdued and sounds like it could have been the start of a major hit for any number of 90s alternative bands. Noel's falsetto when he delivers the line, 'before you start falling', is lovely and is one of the many instances in which Noel would deliver a very different version from Liam's.

'Cloudburst' (N. Gallagher)
B-side to 'Live Forever'
This and 'Sad Song' were released on the Japanese edition of *Definitely Maybe*. In the UK, the only place to hear this was on the 'Live Forever' single. 'Cloudburst' is a fully-formed rocker that would not have sounded out of place on *Definitely Maybe*, but it is hard to make a case for replacing any song on the album with this, given the flow of it already works pretty damn well. The riff that starts at 3:39 is one of the best that Noel ever came up with, and the ending instrumental section is something to behold.

'Supersonic (Live April '94)' (N. Gallagher)
'Thank you, this is the last one. And it's gonna be the single, so go and buy it', is Liam's introduction to this terrific version of a terrific song.

'I Am The Walrus (Live At Glasgow Cathouse, June '94)' (J. Lennon and P. McCartney)
B-side to 'Cigarettes & Alcohol'
An absolute masterpiece of an EP from start to finish, the 'Cigarettes & Alcohol' single would rank towards the top of any ranking of the Oasis singles catalogue. When fans talk about the magic of Oasis B-sides and how they are often 'better than the A-sides', this is where that period starts, and then would continue through the next five singles before some inconsistencies would creep in. Many fans would likely refer to the song 'Cigarettes & Alcohol' as the weakest of the four tracks here.

Oasis never hid their love of The Beatles, especially John Lennon, and 'I Am The Walrus' was a mainstay of their concerts during all eras of the band, and was, fittingly, the last song the band would ever perform on stage together at what turned out to be their final gig in 2009. Originally released by The Beatles in 1967 and never performed live, Oasis were able to make this cover their own. The ending, especially, became something of a highlight at any Oasis gig, with Liam exiting the stage first, followed by Noel, who would put his guitar down and leave the effects on, before then directing the others to 'keep it going for as long as possible'. Perhaps this version goes on a minute, even two minutes, too long, but it still works magnificently.

The credits would list this version as coming from the Glasgow Cathouse in June 1994, but the truth of the matter was far different. This version came from the soundcheck at the Gleneagles Hotel Sony Seminar when no one was present. The crowd noise is allegedly taken from an old bootleg of a Faces concert. There *did* exist a version from the Glasgow Cathouse, which sounded similar, but Noel would ultimately describe it as sounding like shit.

'Listen Up' (N. Gallagher)
B-side to 'Cigarettes & Alcohol'
You could be forgiven for initially assuming you were listening to an outtake of 'Supersonic', given the similarity of the opening guitar riff, with the drums sounding almost exactly like 'Live Forever'. Yet, here we are with one of the great early Oasis B-sides, of which there are many. Oasis released some of the best songs of their career on the 'Cigarettes & Alcohol', 'Whatever' and 'Some Might Say' singles, all released in a six-month period before *(What's the Story) Moring Glory?* hit shelves. 'Listen Up' manages to sound somewhat similar to several key *Definitely Maybe* tracks, but is so damn enjoyable and catchy that it winds up being one of the most effective Oasis songs.

The lyrical themes explored on 'Listen Up' are ones that were becoming very familiar, Noel having written the lyrics in the kitchen at the Maison

Rouge recording studio as part of an eight-hour lyric-writing session, while the rest of the band were still out partying. The tracks on *Definitely Maybe* and its associated B-sides explore Noel's desire to get far away from his current life, both literally and figuratively, and that theme continues here:

> One fine day
> Gonna leave you all behind
> I wouldn't be so bad
> If I had more time

Liam was reaching heights in his vocal delivery that he had seldom reached before, while musically, this is a guitar-heavy song; Noel flexes his inner Neil Young with a guitar break lasting over a minute in length, which was eventually edited for release on *The Masterplan*, albeit by just a few bars. Fans were able to vote on the B-sides they wanted on *The Masterplan* and...

> ...It was one of the ones people voted for a lot... I can see now that was the start of the prog rock phase where I was gonna just chuck guitar solos over everything because I had a brand new guitar that day, and by golly, I'm gonna use it.

Performed intermittently over the years, notably by Noel Gallagher acoustically in 2006, and then again as part of the High Flying Birds, this is an essential song in the Oasis legend.

'Fade Away' (N. Gallagher)
B-side to 'Cigarettes & Alcohol'
Where most B-sides would have paled in the shadows of 'Listen Up', 'Fade Away' is at least an equal, forming a 1-2 punch that is tough to beat. One of the fastest songs in their catalogue, 'Fade Away' sees Liam deliver perhaps his fastest vocal delivery, yet he nails it. The song was slated to appear on *Definitely Maybe* before Noel vetoed it, likely to free up space for 'Slide Away'. Lyrically, 'Fade Away' sees Noel returning to once-again familiar lyrical territory as he talks about growing up, but at the time, not growing old, to take his words from *The Masterplan* liner notes. On a more universal level, one could say this was simply a wake-up call to fans to remember to live their life to the fullest, as was his desire.

Many people have heard melodic similarities between this and 'Freedom' by Wham!, with Noel swearing that any similarities were not intentional. Oasis played 'Fade Away' consistently throughout their career and Noel also performs a terrific stripped-down acoustic version, with the lyrics of the song giving the title to Noel's first solo release *The Dreams We Have as Children – Live at The Royal Albert Hall*, taken from a performance in March 2007.

'Whatever' (N. Gallagher)
A-Side single. Released: 18 December 1994. UK: 3

A monumental, consequential and all-around big deal in the career of Oasis, 'Whatever' was the strategic Christmas single of 1994, Noel knowing he had a good one on his hands. The rate at which Oasis was writing and releasing good songs in 1994 was incredibly impressive and this serves as the icing on that cake. 'Whatever' acts as the official bridge between their first and second albums, one of the only stand-alone singles the band would release. Richard Bowes writes:

> 'Whatever' was one of Noel's oldest songs, written long before the band had a record deal, and had been rehearsed along with other unreleased tracks such as 'All Around The World' at their practice rooms at the Boardwalk. Presumably, it wasn't selected for inclusion on the debut album because there wasn't the budget to record it.

Tony McCarroll, also referring to the fact that the song had been sitting around for years, talked about the band being incredibly tight at this point, being able to predict what one another was going to do and play next in any jam session. A slightly ironic statement, given that the end of McCarroll's time with Oasis was fast approaching. The most notable aspect of 'Whatever' is the strings, arranged by Noel and Nick Ingman. Once we get past the opening acoustic strumming, which sounds like any American alternative song on the radio in 1994, the strings enter at 0:12 and drive the melody and arrangement for the remainder of the song. Ingman would recall Noel sang him the melody of what he wanted the strings to sound like. He had the vision and the sound in his head, but he needed Ingman to nail down the mechanics.

While this is as stately a Noel ballad as he would ever write, there are more movements and themes found within 'Whatever' than almost any other Oasis song. The last half of the song is all instrumental, every instrument slowly and eventually dropping out until we are just left with stately strings, evoking a wedding reception vibe. Finally, the track ends with claps and woos of those in the studio during the recording.

Details and theories vary, but most cite Noel's childhood as the impetus for the lyrics. Some feel it is about Liam and how he was given more freedom as a child than Noel and Paul were, thereby free to do 'whatever'. Others suggest that it is about Noel being taken to work with his dad and realising he did not want to follow in his dad's footsteps.

Not played live as often as one might hope, the most famous performance is the Main Road performance from 1996, replete with a 40-piece brass section. The logistics of playing 'Whatever' live and doing it justice with the strings would have been difficult. Additionally, 'Whatever' became the latest Oasis song to be tethered to another plagiarism suit. English musician Neil Innes released an album in 1973 titled *How Sweet To Be An Idiot* and the title track contains a melody (queue it up to 0:40) on the line 'I'm free to be an idiot' that is very similar to 'Whatever'. Innes was granted a songwriting credit on the song and, as such, it hasn't appeared on as many compilations as it may have otherwise, Noel not wanting to share any royalties and all. It does, however, appear on *Time Flies…1994-2009*.

The Japanese EP version of 'Whatever' would contain the B-sides from 'Cigarettes & Alcohol' and the UK 'Whatever' single.

'(It's Good) To Be Free' (N. Gallagher)
B-side to 'Whatever'

One of three tracks recorded at the Congress House Studio in Austin, Texas. This track, as well as 'Half The World Away', would appear on the 'Whatever' single, while the third song recorded there, 'Talk Tonight', would sit in wait until the 'Some Might Say' single.

Oasis were playing a show in Austin; the band had some time and Noel had a handful of songs that he wanted to record for use as B-sides. Mary Lester, the assistant studio engineer at The Congress House Studio, recalls the sessions at which these three classic songs were recorded:

> As far as the band goes… it was very apparent that Noel was the talent. Liam was a loud-mouth asshole from moment one. I can remember him ranting like a maniac much of the first day… which I thought was pretty hilarious, even though I only understood about 10% of what he was saying due to his thick accent… Noel seemed quiet but was never rude to me. He spent most of the two-day session in the studio with Owen in the control room, while the rest of the band milled about after the basic tracks were done.

While the band, especially Noel, had problems with Tony's drumming, this is the session in which it really started to become clear that the fit was not going to last much longer. Regarding '(It's Good) To Be Free', it took Tony about six takes to get the drumming right, with Noel shouting instructions at the band, and Tony in particular. Noel is said to have shouted at Tony, 'If you don't get this right, I'm gonna come out of here and kick your head in'. The end product is terrific, with Noel playing some especially blistering lead guitar. Even Tony sounds pretty adequate here, good even. Noel said he began writing this song in a swimming pool before ultimately finishing it off in Las Vegas. Confirming the tense mood in the studio, contrasted with the happy vibe of the song:

> It sounds like we are having a really good time in the studio because we are all laughing. But it wasn't funny at all.

The lyrics feature the title to one of the great live Oasis documents *Live by The Sea*:

Yeah little things they make me so happy
All I want to do is live by the sea

One lyrical theory, based on an interview Noel gave in 1998, suggested that
they were written about Paul Gallagher and his time in prison, and how it
was good to be free upon his release. The ending of the song is also unique
in that it sounds like a circus.

It's another fan-favourite song, not performed live very frequently by Oasis,
but it has become a concert staple for Noel Gallagher's High-Flying Birds.
Given the title, it is hard not to read this as a dig at Liam and Oasis.

'Half The World Away'
B-side to 'Whatever'

Like the 'Cigarettes & Alcohol' B-sides, the accompanying songs on the
'Whatever' single are some of the best Oasis songs. Most fans would include
this gem on their list of essential Oasis B-sides, with this author considering
it one of his top five Oasis B-sides. The organ work alone, especially at the
end, is some of the most powerful Oasis music in its understated beauty.
This was written and recorded at the same time as 'Talk Tonight', which
accounts for the similar vibe of the songs, including the sense of longing in
both. In this case, Noel's longing to be transported half the world away, at
least symbolically, as half the world away could simply mean getting out of
Manchester. Both songs were also recorded at The Congress House Studio in
Austin, Texas, along with '(It's Good) To Be Free'.

Opening with a pleasant acoustic guitar that gives the song a sense of hope,
Noel announces in the first line that he would like to leave this city. Moments
after, he specifies that he's referring to Britain with the line, 'and when I
leave this island, I'll book myself into a soul asylum'. He remains hopeful
throughout:

So what do you say?
You can't give me the dreams that are mine anyway
You're half the world away
I've been lost, I've been found
But I don't feel down

The band, and Noel especially, were having immense problems with Tony's
drumming and several people have pointed out that the sessions at The
Congress House Studio were when things really changed in regards to Tony.
Noel allegedly told Tony, in regards to this song, that he was going nowhere
near the drum kit and proceeded to do the drum work himself. Other versions
of the story have Tony starting out playing the drums before Noel forced Tony
to take a break and then recording the part himself. Tony would assign some
credit to himself regarding the drum shuffle that the song employs, saying that

he suggested adapting it from Burt Bacharach's 'This Guy's In Love With You'. Noel would later say that he was surprised he hadn't been sued yet, given the similarities between the songs. 'Half The World Away' also repurposes some lyrics earlier used on 'Comin' On Strong', which would eventually lead to 'Setting Sun' with the Chemical Brothers. Specifically, as heard in 'Comin' On Strong', 'your body's still young and your mind is very old'.

The track would enjoy a boost in popularity and ubiquity due to its use as the theme song for the BBC sitcom *The Royle Family*. It also happens to be Paul Weller's favourite Oasis song. The fact that a track this good was relegated to B-side status is a testament to Noel's songwriting at its peak. This is a song that Noel would perform as a member of Oasis and that he has continued to play in his post-Oasis career.

'Slide Away' (N. Gallagher)
B-side to 'Whatever'
One of the great Oasis songs, yes, but nothing new here; it is identical to the album version. Its release here, however, would ensure that the 'Whatever' EP included two songs that were longer than six minutes. Another four-song single, another four perfect songs.

(What's The Story) Morning Glory? (1995)

Personnel:
Liam Gallagher: vocals
Noel Gallagher: lead guitar, vocals, Mellotron, piano, E-Bow
Paul 'Bonehead' Arthurs: rhythm guitar, Mellotron, piano
Paul 'Guigsy' McGuigan: the bass player
Alan White: drums, percussion
Lead guitar and backing vocals on 'Champagne Supernova' by Paul Weller
Produced by Noel Gallagher and Owen Morris
Assistant Studio Engineer: Nick Brine
UK release date: 2 October 1995
Chart placings: UK: 1, US: 4

Second albums are typically not as influential, popular, hit-filled or important to a band's story as *(What's The Story) Morning Glory?* was for Oasis. The album would make Oasis one of the most popular bands in British history, not just in the 1990s, and by the end of the decade, *(What's The Story) Morning Glory?* would become the best-selling album of the 1990s in the UK. Any 'Battle of Britpop' that Blur may have 'won' was fleeting. For many in Britain, this album put Oasis head and shoulders above their contemporaries and the songs have since engrained themselves into the culture. *Definitely Maybe* is the easy choice for fan-favourite and best Oasis album, but this album contains the most famous songs. Like *Thriller*, *Hysteria* or *Born In The USA*, every song was at the very least *good* and almost any song could have been a massive hit. Regarding *(What's The Story) Morning Glory?*, Wayne Robbins wrote in 2020:

> Every song is good, half a dozen are great, and two, both mid-tempo, 'Wonderwall' and 'Champagne Supernova', belong on the playlist with 'Hey Jude', 'A Day In The Life' and 'A Whiter Shade Of Pale'.

One of the many great things about *(What's The Story) Morning Glory?* is that the sessions for it were the easiest, most laid back and most productive of any Oasis album. Yet, pretty soon, the band, especially the Gallaghers, would be equally known for drama and shenanigans as they were for great music. A lot of these shenanigans would have to do with public drunkenness and feuds with other British bands. Fourteen months separated this album from *Definitely Maybe*, but those months were filled with a lot of terrific music being released, a lot of terrific songs being written and a lot of concerts. The 'Whatever' single ended 1994 for Oasis, another terrific A-side, with three accompanying B-sides that were excellent, even if 'Slide Away' had already been released. As the band entered 1995, they were firing on all cylinders and Noel had a batch of songs that would even eclipse what he had done throughout 1994. The first single that Oasis would release in 1995, 'Some

37

Might Say' was originally demoed as early as June 1994. When released as a single in April 1995, it quickly cemented its status as yet another one of the great Oasis single releases, containing three of their absolute best B-sides. It would be the first official sign that 1995 was perhaps going to be an even bigger year than 1994. Most of *(What's The Story) Morning Glory?* was recorded in May 1995, with Owen Morris saying that they did about one complete song per day, again stressing the good vibes of the sessions.

As the band entered the studio, the most immediate change was that Tony McCarroll was no longer part of the band, with 'Some Might Say' being the last Oasis track he featured on. Noel had famously said that Tony would not have been able to handle the new songs anyway, given many were softer, requiring more nuance and grace. The band brought Alan White on board, who was playing on *Top Of The Pops* with Oasis within 24 hours of joining the band. In a fun little bit of Oasis trivia, they played 'Some Might Say' twice on the show, the first being McCarroll's final performance and the second being White's first performance. The sound on *(What's The Story) Morning Glory?* is different from *Definitely Maybe* and a lot of that simply comes down to where the band was in their career, even with it happening so quickly. As Noel would say: 'Whilst *Definitely Maybe* is about dreaming of being a pop star in a band, *What's The Story* is about actually *being* a pop star in a band'.

While Oasis could already be said to be an anthemic band, with songs like 'Live Forever' and 'Slide Away' to their name, the songs on the second album are even more anthemic, perfect for stadium sing-alongs. More strings and a wider array of instruments are used, there is an epic closing track, Noel takes the lead vocal on one track and there are instrumental segues between some tracks, which all contribute to a marked shift in the band's sound. Noel was already being referred to as the voice of a generation, and former *NME* editor Steve Sutherland would comment, '...with *Morning Glory,* Noel began to take seriously the notion of being the voice of a generation'.

With hindsight, of course, the speed at which Oasis got so big and all-consumingly popular would ultimately lead to issues. At the time of the album's release, however, fans and many critics were over the moon with the new album. The ones who were not on board, initially, had no choice but to hop on the bandwagon eventually. Containing three generation-defining classics surrounded by fan favourites and album tracks, there is almost no fat on the album. Ten proper tracks and two instrumental snippets bring the total running time to almost exactly 50 minutes. The front half contains three of the four singles released from the album, but many fans will point to the second side as their preferred half. The album works from start to finish in a way that no future Oasis albums would. Like with *Definitely Maybe,* the accolades are many. In 2010, it was voted the best album of the past 30 years at the Brit Awards, it is featured on *Rolling Stone*'s Greatest Albums of All-Time list, and at varying times, has been called one of the best albums ever by various music publications in the UK. From the summer of 1995 and the release of the 'Roll With It' single, through to the moment that the album was released in early October 1995, through to the Knebworth performance in 1996, Oasis became truly ubiquitous in British culture, and often not always in a good way, as those above-mentioned shenanigans would garner as much coverage as the songs themselves. As Matt Pooler would say in his book on Britpop, co-written with Peter Richard Adams, regarding *(What's The Story) Morning Glory?*: '...It wasn't so much an album as a moment'.

'Hello' (N. Gallagher, G. Glitter, M. Leander)

The obvious choice for an album opener, given the title of the song, and the self-aware refrain at the end that would lead to another plagiarism suit. The song opens with acoustic strumming, later to be heard in all its glory on 'Wonderwall'. The song, similar to a glam-rock number, storms out of the gate and never looks back. Everyone is on top form here, especially Alan White, who gets to show off his drumming chops in a great showcase. In an odd way, this song is underrated, despite opening the most famous Oasis album. It was never released as a single and isn't featured on any Oasis compilation, yet it remains one of the many highlights on an album filled with them. Written for *Definitely Maybe*, but held back, Noel would simply describe 'Hello' as 'a great fuckin' tune'.

Noel had perfected his songwriting and arranging methods by this point and would play a song for Liam, often just once on an acoustic guitar. He would show him the words and melody and Liam had an uncanny ability to hear the song once, sing it and nail it, making it his own. His gift for phrasing is perhaps his greatest gift of all. This is a song that Liam has kept in his solo setlists and it continues to sound great. Oasis kept it in their setlist throughout 1995 and 1996, before bringing it back for most of the *Heathen Chemistry Tour*.

The song samples Gary Glitter's 1973 hit 'Hello, Hello, I'm Back Again', which says 'hello, hello, it's good to be back'. On 'Hello', towards the end, Noel's backing vocals are filtered through a megaphone as he announces that, yes, it is good to be back. The fallout from Glitter being added as a songwriter would be an extra 1 million pounds in his bank account as of 2013, according to a story in *The Guardian*.

'Roll With It' (N. Gallagher)

A-side single. Released: 14 August 1995. UK: 2

This is a song that is more famous for the cultural context surrounding it than for the substance of the song itself. The so-called Battle of Britpop centred around this, the second single released from *(What's The Story) Morning Glory?*, and the Blur single 'Country House'. While the controversy was more or less engineered by the record companies, the legend around the Blur vs. Oasis rivalry is one of the more famous chapters in all of Britpop and is a subplot that has been covered ad nauseam in documentaries, articles and books. One of the many ironies in this story is that both of these songs were two of the weaker singles by either band, with many Oasis fans considering 'Roll With It' to be one of their weakest A-sides ever, and perhaps the weakest track on *(What's The Story) Morning Glory?*.

By the summer of 1995, Blur had already released three albums and their fourth record would be released in September. Their previous album, the masterpiece *Parklife*, had gone to number one on the charts. Yet, they had never reached number one on the singles chart, while Oasis reached number one for the first time in April 1995 with 'Some Might Say'. Oasis may have been a more explosive band, who were rising in popularity far quicker, but both bands were essentially equal in terms of popularity as 1995 began, with Blur likely being just a little more popular, given they had been around a lot longer. The media had already been reporting that the two bands were engaged in an intense rivalry, which only caused both bands to begin making disparaging comments about the other. It was a perfect contrast as well, with Oasis touted as a working-class band and Blur being more middle-class and steeped in the art-school tradition. Never mind, then, that at the 1995 Brit Awards, there are plenty of pictures of Oasis members and Blur members getting along quite nicely with one another, and Damon Albarn and Graham Coxon even said some kind words about Oasis – although some have suggested those were sarcastic. Some recollections of spring 1995 have Liam gloating to Damon at a celebration party for the success of 'Some Might Say', while others say that Liam made disparaging comments about Damon's girlfriend, Justine Frischmann. Whatever the details may be, paths were crossed.

The actual so-called Battle of Britpop involved Blur's label Food Records moving the release date for the single 'Country House' to be the same as 'Roll With It', thereby creating a contest to see which single would reach number one. There is more nuance here, too, with both the Oasis and Blur camps essentially working with each other, at least initially, to allow both bands to hopefully get a number one. The so-called battle itself was a win-win for both record companies, as this created an incentive for fans of each respective band to go out and buy the new single, not to mention that both bands monopolised the front pages of music publications for several weeks. Ultimately, 'Country House' would occupy the number one spot and 'Roll With It' would take number two. The spoils of victory were short-lived for Blur, however, as they were already in the process of reinventing themselves as a group. Oasis would soon release a single and an album that would eclipse 'Country House' by leaps and bounds, with the media frenzy created in the Battle of Britpop certainly helping to fuel sales. Coming after the actual chart battle, the low point of the feud would see Noel telling a reporter that he wished Damon Albarn and Alex James would 'catch AIDS and die'. He would later take back the comments, blaming being high on drugs for the statement, as well as the reporter catching him backstage after a concert. Nonetheless,

Damon and Noel buried their feud long ago and dozens of videos circulate online of the two performing music together.

In regards to 'Roll With It', the actual song itself has been described as a meat and potatoes rock song, with most people, including Noel, recognising that it is one of the weaker Oasis offerings of this era. It was the first song that Oasis recorded with new drummer Alan White, and the version released as a single and appearing on *(What's The Story) Morning Glory?* is said to be the first take of the song, although Noel has recently said that he thinks it is the second version that people hear on the record. 'Roll With It' is also the only song on the album that was done live, just like *Definitely Maybe*. Lyrically, the song deals with typical Noel themes of believing in one's self, as he would elaborate on to *Select* magazine:

> It's just a typical Oasis thing. 'Shut up moanin' and fuckin' get on with it...' It's the same sentiments as nearly every song we do... it starts to get a bit boring (laughs), but those are the lyrics I feel comfortable with.

Played consistently by the band throughout their career, with an extended break during the *Don't Believe The Truth* era, 'Roll With It' ultimately forms one of the most famous stories in Oasis lore, but musically, leaves something to be desired.

'Wonderwall' (N. Gallagher)

A-side single. Released: 30 October 1995. UK: 2

A capo across the 2nd fret, an Em7 chord, a G chord, a few other chords that people forget and a couple of strums on each: with this, a beginner guitar player can strum *something* that will sound *somewhat* like what is the most popular Oasis song. Getting it to sound *just like* 'Wonderwall' is another issue and one that has perplexed even adequate guitar players since 1995. Not the best song, not even the most culturally ingrained, not the go-to-sing-along, this wasn't even a number-one single. But this is the song that most people are familiar with, even if they know nothing else of Oasis. From the perspective of this author, when people ask me what songs Oasis sing, in response to me telling them I'm writing a book on the band, a poor imitation of the chorus would typically do the trick.

Not one of Noel's favourites, but a great song by his own admission. It is just as well, as 'Wonderwall' is a showcase for Liam. Noel summarises his feelings about the song:

> Outside of England, it's the one song that we're famous for all over the world, and it annoys the fuck out of me, it's not a fucking rock 'n' roll tune. There's quite a vulnerable statement to it... but they're great chords. When people come up to me and say it's one of the greatest tunes ever written, I think: 'fuckin' hell, have you heard 'Live Forever'? But I can't knock it, man, it's paid for many a fucking night out...

Similar to Noel's feelings, Liam seems to equally despise the song, saying in 2008 that he wants to gag every time he has to sing it. Yet, there are also interviews of him claiming that this is one of his three favourite songs to sing live.

As with other Oasis songs, the inspiration for the song is a little spotty, with Noel saying at varying times that it was written for his girlfriend Meg Matthews, or that it was simply about an imaginary friend. It was originally titled 'Wishing Stone' but was changed to 'Wonderwall' after Noel was listening to *Wonderwall Music* by George Harrison – an instrumental album and Harrison's solo debut released in 1968. The music video was a game-changer for the band, winning the Best Video award at the 1996 Brit Awards, the black and white video was ubiquitous on MTV during 1996.

One of the most notable 'Wonderwall-related moments came at the Glastonbury Festival in 2008. Rapper Jay-Z was one of the headliners and Noel made his displeasure known that a hip-hop artist was headlining a traditionally guitar-orientated music festival. Saying, in part, '…I'm not having hip-hop at Glastonbury. It's wrong'. Jay-Z responded by opening his headlining set with a montage of people, including Noel Gallagher, making disparaging comments about him. From there, he opened his show with 'Wonderwall', featuring a guitar he had strapped around his body as a nod to Noel's comments about Glastonbury being a guitar festival. With Jay-Z clearly not overly familiar with the lyrics, the crowd go ecstatic and end up doing most of the singing.

'Wonderwall' has enjoyed something of a rebirth over the last decade, becoming even more popular on streaming platforms such as Spotify, where it has become one of the most streamed songs of all time. Specifically, in terms of songs that were released pre-2000, some lists have shown it as the most streamed song of all time. For a song that failed to hit number one, certainly an impressive feat.

With 'Live Forever' and 'Don't Look Back In Anger', which are better songs, the awards bestowed on 'Wonderwall' have been a little hyperbolic over the years. At various times, and by various publications, it has been called the greatest British song in history or the second-greatest song of all time, as *Q Magazine* declared in 2006.

'Don't Look Back In Anger' (N. Gallagher)
A-side single. Released: 19 February 1996. UK: 1

Lacking the omnipresence of 'Wonderwall', at least in the few years following the release of *(What's The Story) Morning Glory?*, this has turned into the most famous and, for many people, the greatest Oasis song. In recent years, the song has become something of a national anthem in Britain, especially in the aftermath of the Manchester Arena Bombing in 2017. There are plenty of videos on YouTube showing vigils in which the crowd break into singing 'Don't Look In Anger', as well as versions with Chris Martin and Ariana

Grande, and even a version with Liam himself performing the song acapella at Glastonbury in 2017. When released as a single in February 1996, the song would catapult straight to number one, but when first heard on the album, it was simply one of the highlights.

Like many things in the Oasis universe, part of the catalyst for the track came from John Lennon. During the *Definitely Maybe* Tour, one night in New York, Noel tells the story of someone working for the band who had a brother with a tape of one of the final interviews that John Lennon ever did. On the tape, Lennon says something to the effect of, 'and then they'll tell you that the brains you had have gone to your head'. Noel says that the line stuck with him and he knew he had to work it into a song, and this was also the inspiration for the opening piano in 'Don't Look Back In Anger', being similar to Lennon's 'Imagine'. The song was written in Paris after a night at a strip club, if we are to believe Noel's interviews, with him even going as far as saying that the name Sally was inspired by a stripper. However, there is substantial evidence that it was, in fact, Liam who came up with the 'Sally can wait' line, also garnered from Noel's interviews. Noel has said that Lyla, the titular character from the song of the same name, is said to be Sally's sister. Inspiration for Sally aside, this is not only one of Noel's masterpieces, but it is one of the great songs of the decade. Noel was so smitten when he initially wrote the first draft of the song, that he performed it as a song-in-progress as part of an acoustic set in April 1995. Noel would continue tinkering with the song, before arriving at the full-blown production that is heard on *(What's The Story) Morning Glory?*. By the time of Glastonbury 1995, the song was fully integrated into the setlist, though it was not yet the showstopper it would become.

There are a lot of little moments within this song that make it great and warrant repeat listens. The lead guitar phrases at 0:05, Alan White's drums at 0:34, Noel singing 'stand up beside the fireplace, take that look from off your face' and the strings that slowly increase in volume all lead us into the greatest Oasis chorus of them all at 1:10. At 1:55, Noel sings, 'please don't put your life in the hands...of a rock and roll band', as the guitar dances over the top. The guitar solo, starting at 3:04, is not flashy, but perfectly placed, and Alan White's drum fill at 3:35 takes us to the final two choruses. And, of course, Noel's vocals become high-pitched as he finishes the song:

But don't look back in anger
Don't look back in anger
I heard you say
At least not today

Noel gave Liam the choice between singing this and 'Wonderwall' – Liam chose the latter. Versions do exist of Liam singing 'Don't Look Back In Anger' in the studio, but this song belongs to Noel and the fans, and it is hard to hear anybody else sing it, even Liam. Noel has performed this song live at almost every single concert he has performed since 1995. To call it a highlight of every concert would not do it justice. The song has taken on a meaning, even before 2017, that Noel can't put his finger on:

> I think it came from somewhere else. I think it was a song that was there somewhere, and if I hadn't written it, you know, Bono would have written it... It's like one of those great songs, 'One' and 'Let It Be', and yeah, I did just compare myself to Paul McCartney there. You know, they're there. If they fall out of the sky and land on your lap, lucky you.

There are plenty of famous versions of this song, especially given the tragic events of 2017. There are plenty of powerful versions where Noel only sings the verses but steps away from the mic for the chorus. In July 2009 at Wembley, Noel did not sing a single word in the entire song, he simply let the audience start and finish the song. One of the funny things to watch during these sing-alongs is if the fans are singing 'her soul slides away' *or* 'my soul slides away', with fans often getting confused. The first chorus features 'her soul', and then it switches to 'my' for the remaining three. An essential song in the discography, a life-affirming chorus and, as Noel simply states, 'it's got the magic'.

'Hey Now!' (N. Gallagher)
If any song on *(What's The Story) Morning Glory?* is overlooked, it is 'Hey Now!'. The least known proper song on the album, Noel even recognised it as the one that nobody talks about. Overlooked does not automatically equate with being a bad or good song, as 'Hey Now!' does have its slight charms. If any complaint could be levelled against 'Hey Now!', one could easily argue that it goes on far too long and overstays its welcome by about three minutes. If one was forced to pick a weak link on the record, this would be a contender.

   The musical impetus for 'Hey Now!' was simply a few chords that the band used to jam at soundchecks. Noel is proud of the lyrics and has recently pointed to the lines, 'I took a walk with my fame/down memory lane/I never did find my way back', as being especially strong. Interestingly, Noel points out that the large quantity of lyrics means that this was a song he had written before they arrived at the studio to record the album, the implication being that Noel would have never spent *that* much time on a song once the band were in the studio. Never performed live by the band and despite having its defenders, Noel's assessment that it is the song nobody talks about is pretty spot on.

'Untitled/Swamp Song – Excerpt 1' (N. Gallagher/Oasis)
When originally released on CD, this interlude and the second one were simply referred to as 'Untitled'. Only on re-issues have they been labelled as 'The Swamp Song – Excerpt 1' or 2. And that's all it is. An excerpt from 'The

Swamp Song' that would eventually be released on *The Masterplan*, the first part coming in at 0:44 seconds. It's a bit random, perhaps, but also works well to break up the album and keep people guessing. The sounds heard on 'The Swamp Song' are vastly different from the majority of songs that make up this album, lacking any of their accessibility or catchiness.

'Some Might Say' (N. Gallagher)

A-side single. Released: 24 April 1995. UK: 1

This, their first number-one single, and first single from *(What's The Story) Morning Glory?*, is perhaps the quintessential Britpop song. Noel, in fact, calls it the archetypal Oasis song. What's more, Noel does not view it as being part of *(What's The Story) Morning Glory?*, but as part of the stand-alone EP with 'Talk Tonight', 'Acquiesce' and 'Headshrinker', as it was recorded well before the sessions for the *(What's The Story) Morning Glory?*, hence why Tony McCarroll appears on the record. This would be his last performance on an Oasis song. Acting as a bridge between the debut and their sophomore record, and laid down two months before the sessions for *(What's The Story) Morning Glory?* would start, it really does display Oasis becoming a different band and is, in many ways, the archetypal Britpop song, even though the so-called Battle for Britpop hadn't even started yet. Needless to say, this is also a far stronger song than 'Roll With It'.

Kicking off side two of *(What's The Story) Morning Glory?*, which is somehow even stronger than side one, this begins with one of the Oasis' most famous guitar intros, with the drums not joining until about 17 seconds into the song. It sounds a little jingle-jangly, a little grunge, a little classic rock; at the time, it didn't sound at all like any other Britpop band and it didn't even sound like The Beatles. It was truly a new sound. Sonically, it also doesn't sound like anything else on *(What's The Story) Morning Glory?* given it was recorded before the sessions for the album started and, in this sense, it remains one of the most unique songs in the Oasis canon.

An Oasis fan could do worse than declaring the 'Some Might Say' single as the greatest the band ever released, with only 'Cigarettes & Alcohol' being as beloved among Oasis purists. The three accompanying songs are all excellent, bar none, and when taken as a whole, truly show how effective Oasis were at their peak. Equally impressive is the cover art for the single, created by Brian Cannon with detailed directions from Noel. The cover cleverly displays nearly every lyric uttered in the song, even 'she's got dirty dishes on the brain'.

With some of the best lyrics, at least in the verses, that Noel was writing at the time, the most famous line, by default, has to be, 'Some might say we will find a brighter day', as there is a banner with these words hanging in Etihad Stadium. Released almost a full six months before *(What's The Story) Morning Glory?*, and four months before their next single 'Roll With It', the 'Some Might Say' single was the only new Oasis music that fans heard in the spring and most of the summer of 1995. As Liam would say regarding the song to journalist James Brown for an *Uncut* interview: 'We were 'avin' it, man, on the piss, 'avin' it. They were the days, man, no kids an' that, just go out on a fucking Friday and come back Monday'.

'Cast No Shadow' (N. Gallagher)

'Cast No Shadow' was dedicated to Richard Ashcroft of The Verve after he had dedicated the song 'A Northern Soul' to Noel, with Noel saying:

> He always seemed to me that he was not entirely happy with the things that were happening around him. So the lyrics, 'bound with all the weight of all the words he tried to say', was cos I always felt that he'd been born in the wrong place at the wrong time, and always tried to say the right things, but they went wrong. When I first sang the song to him, he was near tears.

It would be hard to call the song overlooked, as it appears on the most popular British album of the decade, yet it has never appeared on an Oasis compilation, was never released as a single and was not played live after 2002, where it was only performed once. Still, fans often cite this song as being amongst the strongest of the era, and it is a clear highlight of the second half of *(What's The Story) Morning Glory?*

Noel has said that he initially wanted the song to sound like Pink Floyd, as the chords are very similar to 'Wish You Were Here'. He would later criticise the song for sounding half-baked and criticise himself for not being able to decide what kind of song it wanted to be, saying it was a little bit country. Although Noel, like John Lennon before him, was not always the best judge of his own music. Noel did rightfully point to the lyrics as being some of his best:

> Bound with all the weight of all the words he tried to say
> Chained to all the places that he never wished to stay

In classic Noel fashion, he has no recollection of writing the words. The song becomes a showcase for Liam's singing, which is terrific throughout the record, and features Noel delivering some of his famous backing vocals. Noel tended to sing more of the acoustic-based songs in the catalogue and it is nice to hear Liam taking centre stage on this one – fans may have wished for more of Liam's lead vocals on the more acoustic-based tracks.

Both Liam and Noel have performed the song as solo artists, with Liam delivering a showstopping performance as part of his MTV Unplugged performance. Richard Ashcroft and Noel would have a minor feud in 2018 when Noel listed him as one of the stars who used an 'army of songwriters' to help him write songs. Ashcroft was unhappy, Liam defended Ashcroft and it made for a few fun days of minor headlines.

'She's Electric' (N. Gallagher)

It would be easy to call this the weakest song on the album, occupying the same role that 'Digsy's Dinner' serves on *Definitely Maybe*. However, 'She's Electric' has many charms and actually ranks very high on polls asking for favourite/best Oasis songs. It is infectious and catchy as hell, with some damn funny lyrics.

Written for *Definitely Maybe,* but replaced by its sister song 'Digsy's Dinner', which sounded better live as it was a less complicated song. Liam hits some of his best high notes in the song and the whole vibe is very Britpop and 1960s. Never becoming a mainstay of the setlist, even in 1995, 'She's Electric' was played on the *Heathen Chemistry* Tour before being dropped. Noel Gallagher has performed it as a solo artist, somewhat randomly, and it is unlikely Liam would ever touch it again because of the high notes. Can I be electric too?

'Morning Glory' (N. Gallagher)

Few sounds are more exciting to an Oasis fan than the helicopter noises that kick off 'Morning Glory'. 'When he sings the first line, you know you're at a gig... that's why we always play it early on', Noel says of one of the great Oasis rockers. This is a song about drugs, influenced by drugs. Never one to be consumed by the depth of lyrics, Noel's words were often simply a means to get the engine started, as he would put it.

Noel says he took the title from a girl he used to see in America, and she would say to him in a somewhat annoying way, 'what's the story, morning glory?' Of course, the fun implication is that morning glory refers to a morning erection, but perhaps this female friend was referring to the Morning Glory flower. Noel remains confused as to why it became the title of the album, which is slightly ironic given how famous both the album and song have become.

The only plausible complaint about the song is that it would have been nice to have a proper second verse. Perhaps this was Noel's way of expressing the effects of drugs on his psyche at the time, the repetitiveness, etc. There is an obvious Beatles reference in the lyric, 'walking to the sound of my favourite tune, Tomorrow never knows what it doesn't know too soon'. This also fits with the drug references – living day to day, constantly using drugs.

On an album that is dominated by ballads and mid-tempo songs, this is the most ferocious rocker on the album and reminds listeners that Oasis could rock as hard, if not even harder, than they did on *Definitely Maybe*. Surprising no one, this song became a mainstay of the setlist and was essentially performed at every Oasis show from 1995 onward, usually serving as a highlight of the early part of the show. While not released as a single in the UK, it is one of the most famous and beloved songs in the catalogue and rightfully occupies a spot on the *Stop The Clocks* compilation.

'Untitled/Swamp Song – Excerpt 2' (N. Gallagher/Oasis)

'Morning Glory' segues into the second instrumental interlude on the album. This one teases the underwater sounds that feature at the beginning of ...

'Champagne Supernova' (N. Gallagher)

The same underwater sounds are quickly joined by a relaxing acoustic guitar accompanied by subdued lead lines – the listener immediately knows that they are in for something special. It was released as a single in the US, but not in the UK, where it was a mainstay on MTV throughout 1996 and 1997. Alongside 'Wonderwall', this is typically one of two songs that the average American non-Oasis fan knows about. What's more, this is perhaps the archetypal example of people not knowing what Noel is talking about in his songs. But that, in and of itself, is one of Noel's greatest talents. Sure, it's impossible to walk down a hall faster than a cannonball, but almost everyone of a certain age knows that lyric. Furthermore, who can even say what a 'Champagne Supernova' is? Yet, once you hear the song, the scale of it, the multiple guitar solos and perhaps Liam's greatest vocal performance, it would be impossible to call the song anything else. Regarding the lyrics, Noel had a terrific response when a writer was bugging him about the confusion that the lyrics provoke: '...but are you telling me, when you've got 60,000 singing it, they don't know what it means? It means something different to every one of them'.

There are two guitar solos just in the second half of the song, with Paul Weller playing one of them and also adding in some backing vocals for good measure. Paul Weller was a legend because of his time in The Jam, writing some of the greatest songs of the late 1970s and early 1980s before joining The Style Council, where he remained for much of the 1980s. He was enjoying a resurgence in the mid-1990s, in large part due to the success and quality of his 1993 solo album *Wild Wood*. By the time that he appeared on 'Champagne Supernova', his cultural clout was immense.

Steve Baltin of *Cashbox* would say of the American single release:

'Champagne Supernova' overflows the songwriting talents of Noel Gallagher. Oasis is proving time and time again that there isn't another rock act out there that can touch the group as a singles band.

This was likely their biggest hit in America, hitting number one on the Modern Rock chart, and for a moment, it seemed as if Oasis was about to blow up in America, especially with this and 'Wonderwall'. Ultimately, it was not to be, although those two songs engrained themselves into the minds of most Americans who came of age during the 1990s. There would have been no other way to end *(What's The Story) Morning Glory?* and 'Champagne Supernova' has rightly taken its place as one of the great Oasis songs. Played at most concerts and also played by both Liam and Noel as solo artists, this appears on *Familiar To Millions* and *Stop The Clocks*.

And with that, one of the most famous albums in British history ends. It is the easy answer when asked what the best Oasis album is, and when listening from front to back, it is hard to argue against it being anything other than a masterpiece. When taken alongside *Definitely Maybe*, the majority of beloved Oasis songs exist on those two albums, and certainly comprise the classic era of the band and the peak of Noel's songwriting, especially with the B-sides accounted for. The B-sides that accompanied the four singles from *(What's The Story) Morning Glory?* make up the strongest that Noel would ever write and lead to the inevitable what-ifs regarding if they all had been saved for a third album. While those questions make for great late-night fodder, the fact that they appear on these Oasis singles is part of the lore and fans would have it no other way.

(What's The Story) Morning Glory B-Sides/EPs
'Talk Tonight' (N. Gallagher)
B-side to 'Some Might Say'

The first of the beloved B-sides on the 'Some Might Say' EP, this is a lovely Noel-sung ballad recorded at The Congress House Studio in Austin, Texas, in the fall of 1994. Recorded the morning after they did '(It's Good) To Be Free', Noel was wrapping up the final touches on the song, and within two hours, it was completed and recorded. Owen Morris would recall that the rest of the band showed up to the studio after it had already been laid down, with Tony McCarroll nowhere to be found on this track or 'Half The World Away', which they would record immediately after. Noel's favourite part of the recording is the sound of him taking his watch off and coughing at the beginning – as he put it, it sounds really honest.

It was inspired by real events, notably, the near-breakup of Oasis. On their first tour of America, Noel and 'the singer' had a falling out, 'funnily enough' he remarks in the same breath. A mixed-up setlist, Liam snorting crystal meth and Noel operating on little-to-no sleep all contributed to what was, by all accounts, a horrible concert. Here is where things get a little fuzzy, as multiple versions of this story exist. Packing up his passport and his bags, Noel fled to Las Vegas, staying at the Luxor Hotel in the Pharaoh suite, with about six grand to burn. While some details are shaky, Noel winds up back in San Francisco, where he contacts Melissa Lim, whom he had befriended earlier. She keeps him company for a few days as she accompanies him on walks, tours of record stores, music listening and a trip to Huntingdon Park. Their time also included grabbing several music magazines, and when he opened up a copy of *Melody Maker*, which showed an upcoming string of shows in the UK – all of which were sold out – she told him he'd be nuts to give this up as 'it's blowing up over there', despite anything happening (or not) in America. While the story itself has grown in legend over the years, and Noel himself has said he would have gone back to Oasis whether or not he met the woman – 'what the fuck are they going to do without me?',

49

he quipped – she still provided some much-needed grounding for Noel and helped inspire one of the loveliest songs in the Oasis canon. Noel claims not to remember Lim's name in the documentary *Oasis: Supersonic*, which gives fans the great quote from Lim herself: 'Keith Richards can remember the name of his milkman from when he was eight years old. I don't know what's going on with Noel, and that's fine. I was part of something that touched so many people. That's good enough'.

The first line in the song, 'sitting on my own, chewing on a bone', is about doing too much cocaine, too far away from home, a sentiment which Noel has expressed in his lyrics many times. Perhaps the most famous line in the song deals with Snapple Strawberry Lemonade, a favourite of Melissa's: 'All your dreams are made of strawberry lemonade, and you make sure I eat today'. The guitar playing, especially in the chorus when Noel does his light hammer-ons, really makes this song. Noel was coming into his own as a singer in 1995, becoming more confident, and on these ballads, he really was able to deliver them perfectly.

A mainstay of Oasis setlists during their peak popularity, Noel would often play 'Talk Tonight' as part of a mini-acoustic set. He continues to play it as part of the High Flying Birds. It was one of the few B-sides that showed up on *Stop The Clocks*.

'Acquiesce' (N. Gallagher)
B-side to 'Some Might Say'
And we have arrived at yet another song that many fans consider to be the greatest Oasis achievement. This is their ultimate display of brotherly love, at least in how fans perceive it, and the pinnacle of the Gallagher brothers working together to create a masterpiece. Beginning with a preview, of sorts, of their upcoming album with snippets of 'Morning Glory', the song quickly segues into one of their crunchiest riffs. This is a song about friendship in the truest sense of the word and it is incredibly tempting to read it as a conversation between Liam and Noel. Liam asks at various points:

I don't know what it is
That makes me feel alive
I don't know how to wake
The things that sleep inside
I only want to see the light
That shines behind your eyes

And Noel, responding to his brother:

Because we need each other
We believe in one another

And I know we're going to uncover
What's sleepin' in our soul

Noel has said before that it is about him and Liam, and when Noel sings, 'cause we need each other, we believe in one another', it's impossible not to think that he's singing about his brother. In other interviews, however, he says it's not about Liam or brotherhood in any sense at all. Noel recalls writing the song on the train and going to Loco Studios to record 'Some Might Say', which would appear as the A-side single. The train got stuck for several hours; Noel recalls some type of signal failure, yet with his guitar in tow, he was able to write the entire melody while stuck waiting for the train to move. When Alan McGee heard the song, he insisted that it had to be a single, whereas Noel felt 'Some Might Say' was the stronger song. In the end, Noel got his way and simply did the opposite of what the record company man suggested, relegating the song to exalted B-side status.

It's a show-stopping performance every time it's played live, despite Liam typically forgetting the second verse and simply repeating the first verse. It has been played consistently at concerts since 1995, save for *The Tour Of Brotherly Love* in 2001 and the *Dig Out Your Soul* tour. Neither Gallagher brother has performed it as a solo artist, making it one of the few canonical Oasis songs not performed live in any of the solo iterations. Consequently, it becomes all the more special as the brothers are seemingly unable to perform it unless *together*. In Noel's song-by-song analysis in *The Masterplan* liner notes, he has some great quotes about 'Acquiesce', including this:

Liam couldn't sing the chorus for some reason. I think he was drunk or something, but he couldn't get the high notes. So I decided to sing it. When the record came out, everyone was going, 'It's a song about Liam', and that I was saying we need each other, we believe in one another – which was total fucking bullshit. It wasn't about that, but 'cos he was singing the verses and I was singing the choruses, people were like: 'Oh God man, the two brothers are, like, sharing their love for each other, even though they hate each other. It's just like, wow, they're bonding on record'. Haha! So, we went along with that for ages!

'Headshrinker' (N. Gallagher)
B-side to 'Some Might Say'
This is the heaviest of the three singles on 'Some Might Say', and certainly one of the most punk rock-sounding things they ever did. You could be forgiven for thinking you were listening to an AOR track from the mid-1970s, with a killer, floating bassline throughout. The only potential similarity is 'Bring It On Down', the most punk-influenced song from *Definitely Maybe*. As Noel would describe it, the intention was to sound like The Faces on speed. Another terrific Liam vocal performance, 'Headshrinker' was written about

a girl that Liam was dating at the time, despite Noel having no idea what a headshrinker was, simply assuming it was some type of psychiatrist:

> I know a girl who's lost and lonely
> Sits by the phone on her own
> But the phone don't ring
> And the birds don't sing in her tree

The titular headshrinker followed the band everywhere, according to Noel, and was a general pain in the arse. Presumably sitting by the phone, alone because she has no friends, waiting for a call that never comes, and the lack of birds, or intelligence, in her tree has made her insufferable. After a dozen or so performances in 1995, the song was only played one other time; Noel had essentially forgotten about the song until the sessions for *Be Here Now* when Owen Morris was playing a slew of old songs for Noel. Noel heard this one, remembered how great it was, and unilaterally decided it was going on *The Masterplan*, even if the fans did not vote for it.

'It's Better People' (N. Gallagher)
B-side to 'Roll With It'
'Cigarettes & Alcohol', 'Whatever' and 'Some Might Say' comprised a killer three-single run, with every B-side being essential. We see a slight dip in quality here as The 'Roll With It' single is, of course, most famous for the pseudo showdown with Blur and the songs are likely the weakest, top to bottom, of the era, with 'Roll With It' itself one of the weaker A-sides. The first B-side on the single, 'It's Better People' is the weakest of the lot, which is relative, as it is still a solid tune. This layered acoustic song is catchy and has a great melody. A scroll through some Oasis message boards yields several theories about the lyrics, which posit it as being about a homosexual relationship. While Noel is, of course, free to write lyrics about anything he wants, a more likely theory is simply that Noel wanted to write a joyous song that was rooted somewhat in a 1960s utopian theme, which is something he would return to several times over in the next couple of years. Rarely played live, this is one that Noel resurrected and performed live on several stops in 2016. Not chosen for release on *The Masterplan*, this is one of the few B-sides from the era that languishes in relative obscurity.

'Rockin' Chair' (N. Gallagher)
B-side to 'Roll With It'
The highlight of the 'Roll With It' release, including the A-side itself and a no-brainer for release on *The Masterplan*, this track has a melody that won't quit and contains another canonical Liam vocal performance. This is another track about the desire to get out of town as, with age, the narrator yearns to fly the nest. It also features a lovely acoustic guitar solo, coming right after the

initial chorus. Bumped off of *(What's The Story) Morning Glory?* in favour of 'Wonderwall', which is a hard decision to argue against, this is another song that was too good to be relegated to B-side status.

The lyrical themes that Noel is exploring here had been explored on at least a dozen other Oasis tracks written around this time, but that did not matter when the performance was this good: 'I'm older than I wish to be/This town holds no more for me'.

Along with 'Columbia', this is one of the songs in which there was controversy between Noel and Chris Griffiths regarding who wrote what and who wrote how much. Ultimately, a settlement was made and Griffiths did receive royalties.

Only played live sparingly, as Liam struggled with the high notes in the chorus. Another essential playlist addition.

'Live Forever (Live At Glastonbury '95)' (N. Gallagher)
B-side to 'Roll With It'
In 1995, 'Live Forever' was not yet the universal anthem it would become, but it was damn popular and ubiquitous, and this is a good version serving as an effective showcase for the band, even if Noel's background vocals are a bit wobbly.

'Round Are Way' (N. Gallagher)
B-side to 'Wonderwall'
A celebrated tune yet one that flies a little under the radar as it was not included on *The Masterplan*. This is a poppy, horn-heavy song with clunky lyrics and an overall feel of joy – this is Noel's best take on a 60s psychedelic tune. Ostensibly a song about Manchester and growing up, with mentions of a paper boy, a teacher, the letterbox and birds singing, it reads as a slice-of-life narrative. Even though there were a lot of terrific songs to choose from, excluding this from *The Masterplan* is one of the few potential complaints that can be made of that album. This was played in 1995 and 1996 by Oasis, perhaps most famously by Noel for MTV Unplugged, before being dropped and picked up very intermittently by Noel on his solo tours. The title features a deliberate typo, likely a tribute to Slade, a band whom Oasis loved and who would often misspell song titles.

'The Swamp Song' (N. Gallagher)
B-side to 'Wonderwall'
(What's The Story) Morning Glory? contained two brief instrumental snippets that fans would soon learn were simply culled from 'The Swamp Song', as the 'Wonderwall' single came out a few weeks after the album. A great little rocker, this is a romp with loud guitars and one of the first songs the band ever jammed on with Alan. Originally called 'The Jam', Noel thought it should be changed after it was decided that Paul Weller would play on the song,

given he was already in the studio for 'Champagne Supernova'. One of Noel's favourite songs and a terrific show-opener, this would eventually be replaced by the terrific future track 'Fuckin' In The Bushes'.

'The Masterplan' (N. Gallagher)
B-side to 'Wonderwall'
An exceptional song that Liam laments not having sung. Noel has said his biggest regret is relegating this song to a B-side, which perhaps explains why the essential album of Oasis B-sides is titled *The Masterplan*. He would elaborate on this in his 'Lock The Box' interview:

> One of my favourite songs of *my* songs… there are certain songs, for me, that are great, but then there are the chosen few where you really fuckin nail it… like the words, the melody, the structure… that's one of them.

It was determined that 'Wonderwall' was going to be the third single from *(What's The Story) Morning Glory?*. At this point in time, Noel had written two critically acclaimed LPs and almost two dozen B-sides of remarkably consistent quality. What's more, he says he already had the songs that would become *Be Here Now* earmarked but was still fine-tuning them. Every Oasis single up to that point had four songs on it: the single itself, plus three other songs. When it came time for the 'Wonderwall' single to be released, Noel needed one more song. A session was booked in Maison Rouge in Fulham and there was one day to record a song. Noel said he entered the studio and this is what came out. Upon Alan McGee hearing it, he felt it was simply too good to be released as a B-side, with Noel simply assuring him that he doesn't write shit songs.

Noel plays both guitar and bass on the track, with his acoustic strumming and bass playing entering ten seconds into the track, giving way to the most pronounced strings on an Oasis track since 'Whatever'. The song sounds epic and certainly wasn't what most bands were putting out, tucked away on track four on the third single release from a sophomore album. At just over a minute in, Noel begins delivering the lyrics. Following the first chorus, the song features a backwards guitar solo, which feels jaggedly psychedelic, and, while an easy studio trick, adds a nice touch to the tune. The second verse contains more Noel-isms, such as the evergreen, 'There's four and twenty million doors on life's endless corridor', before another chorus. After the second chorus, guitars and strings are layered on top of each other, bringing to mind 'Champagne Supernova'. The last minute of the song is an extended fade-out with the main theme being played again, and for a brief moment, Noel can be heard singing 'Octopus's Garden'. Perhaps the only complaint one could levy against the tune is that it would have been nice to hear one more chorus during the extended fade.

There are some Noel-sung tracks that may leave listeners wishing to hear a vocal interpretation by Liam, with the end conclusion sometimes being that

Liam's voice may have been better suited. It's hard to imagine anyone singing this as well as Noel does. Liam gets the last word: 'Big tune, man. Good words. What's it about? Haven't a clue'.

'Step Out' (Gallagher, Wonder, Cosby, Moy)
B-side to 'Don't Look Back In Anger'
1996 was a monumental year for Oasis in terms of concerts, media coverage, controversy, songwriting, collaboration and the future of the band. As for official releases, however, all we have is the 'Don't Look Back In Anger' single, which means there are really only three new Oasis songs that the public would hear in 1996. One of those was this damn near irresistible little B-side which led to another songwriter controversy. The song bears a similarity to the Stevie Wonder song 'Uptight (Everything's Alright)', and, as such, was removed from *(What's The Story) Morning Glory?*. While tempting to imagine where it would have fitted on the album, it likely would have messed up the flow of the record. It's a high-energy rocker that Noel sings, even though the tempo was custom-built for Liam and, in fact, there exists a version with Liam singing that is terrific. Played live a handful of times on the *Standing On The Shoulder Of Giants* Tour, and included on certain pressings of *Familiar To Millions*, this is great rocker from the era, with a formula that would be repeated several times on subsequent records.

'Underneath The Sky' (N. Gallagher)
B-Side to 'Don't Look Back In Anger'
An average B-side that wound up on *The Masterplan* but is not talked about much. Interestingly, the song features Noel and Bonehead playing the piano together.

> We needed one more track. It's a little like 'Dead End Street' by The Kinks in the middle. It's not identical, but I always liked that bit. So, I think I got that bit first and wrote the verses around that. The piano bit is Bonehead playing the high bits and me playing the low bits. Being left-handed, I have always wanted to build a left-handed piano; to me, it would be more natural, which is why I never play piano. On this one, I just play only two notes like that and he plays the rhythm bit.

This was only performed live once by Oasis, which is likely wise, as the background vocals, not to mention the piano work, would have been difficult to pull off convincingly in a live setting.

'Cum On Feel The Noize' (Holder, Lea)
B-side to 'Don't Look In Anger'
A terrifically fun cover for both listeners and the band, creating a party atmosphere like few other songs in their canon. Noel says this was one of the

first songs he learnt on guitar, as it is an easy one for novice players. They closed their famous Maine Road shows with this song, before retiring it. It could have served as a great encore, yet it hides away as the final B-side from *(What's The Story) Morning Glory?* and, as such, brings the era to a close.

'You've Got To Hide Your Love Away' (Lennon, McCartney)

This is a song that Noel could have likely played at the drop of a hat, and that is probably what happened. It was released on the 'Some Might Say' single in Japan, along with the demo version of 'Some Might Say', making it a major collector's item. Originally released by The Beatles on the *Help!* album, this Lennon composition was part of a 'Dylan period' according to the composer himself. This was the first Beatles track to feature an outside musician, with John Scott playing tenor and alto flutes. No one plays flute on the Oasis version, but Noel does hum the melody of the flute, which adds a fun touch. This is a relatively short and easy song to cover and play, and that's exactly what Noel delivers here. A little over two minutes in length, there are no other instruments, just Noel and an acoustic guitar. It won't make anyone forget The Beatles' version, but it's a relatively forgotten Oasis cover that is now easy to find as part of the deluxe remastered edition of *(What's The Story) Morning Glory?*

'Bonehead's Bank Holiday' (N. Gallagher)

While certainly a relative statement to make, Bonehead is the most famous member of Oasis, whose last name is not Gallagher. It is also likely that he was the most musically talented member of the band, he just lacked songwriting chops. As such, despite being in a band that became popular beyond his wildest dreams, he arguably never got to really spread his wings. This is *not* a song he gets to spread his wings on, but it is a song which gives him the distinction of being the only Oasis member to have a song named after him. This is his Ringo moment, purposely written for Bonehead to give him a track to sing. It is also a fan favourite, if only for Bonehead's offbeat vocal delivery and containing irreverent lyrical gems like:

She said her name was Dot
She didn't half talk a lot

Of all the Oasis songs, however, there was no statement to be made here, no anthemic chorus, just five guys having fun. The studio banter at the end of the track is amusing, especially when they go back into the 'la la la's. Many journalists and fans have pointed out that the track has a bit of a Blur vibe and sounds similar to Blur music that was being made around this time, which is not untrue. Initially a relatively obscure song and not easily accessible, it was included on the deluxe remastered edition of *(What's The Story) Morning Glory?*

Be Here Now (1997)

Personnel:
Liam Gallagher: vocals
Noel Gallagher: guitar, backing vocals
Bonehead: guitar
Guigsy: bass
Whitey: drums, percussion
Mike Rowe: keyboards
Johnny Depp: slide guitar on 'Fade In-Out'
Mark Coyle: backwards bits on 'D'You Know What I Mean?'
Mark Feltham: harmonica on 'All Around The World'
Strings arranged by Nick Ingram and Noel Gallagher
All songs by Noel Gallagher (Oasis Music/Creation Songs Ltd/Sony/ATV Music Publishing)
Produced by Owen Morris and Noel Gallagher
Recording engineer: Nick Brine
Mastered by Mike Marsh at The Exchange
Recorded at Abbey Road, Ridge Farm, Air, Master Rock and Orinoco Studios, England between November 1996 and April 1997
UK release date: 21 August 1997
Chart placings: UK: 1, US: 2

The Knebworth 1996 performance was perhaps the defining moment in the history of Oasis. What many fans do not realise, and certainly did not realise at the time, is that Noel had written almost every song that would appear on *Be Here Now*, which was released in August 1997 before that 1996 performance. The songs were initially recorded as near fully formed demos in May 1996 when Noel went on a holiday in the Caribbean island of Mustique, shacking up at Mick Jagger's home there. Meg Matthews was present for much of the time, as was Johnny Depp and his girlfriend at the time, Kate Moss. These demos, The Mustique Sessions, would eventually see release on the 2016 deluxe reissue of *Be Here Now*. The story goes that Noel was in Mustique for two weeks before calling up Owen Morris to ask him to bring an eight-track and a drum machine for Noel to nail the demos down. Morris recalled how happy he would have been to get just two songs nailed down. Instead, Noel laid down 15 songs, the bones of which would remain pretty much identical to what was later heard on *Be Here Now*. To the regret of Owen Morris, the demos were not used and referenced to the extent that they perhaps should have been in hindsight. It has become something of a common lament amongst certain fans that the demos themselves were not simply released as the third studio Oasis album, though obviously some normal polishing would have been required.

1996 also saw the Noel Gallagher collaboration with The Chemical Brothers, 'Setting Sun', based on an old Oasis song, 'Comin' On Strong'. The end product would be compared to The Beatles' masterpiece, 'Tomorrow Never Knows', as journalists had to continue to find Beatles comparisons and references.

Many people, including Noel, have commented that the 1996 Knebworth performance was a pinnacle that could never be matched, and in hindsight, the band could have called it quits. They had accomplished what they set out to do and got there faster than most bands in history. Noel, however, began to lose his muse and the well of songs that had been bursting was now drying up. They got through the infamous sessions for *Be Here Now*, did their biggest tour ever and Noel was ready to call it quits. An oversimplified version of the problems that Oasis experienced during the sessions for *Be Here Now* can be boiled down to a few factors: unlimited time and money, changing band dynamics, drug usage and minor apathy from Noel. On top of that, public opinion was turning a bit against Oasis in 1997. The crazy height of their celebrity status was beginning to work against them, and 1996 saw very little new music and a lot of outlandish news stories being published about the band, with an obvious focus on the Gallagher brothers, especially Liam. As such, journalists and fans were less focused on any latest single than they were on Liam's house hunting or Noel quitting the band 'again'. In hindsight, it's relatively clear to see that *Be Here Now* was going to be a let-down, even if the songs were significantly stronger than some naysayers said.

Yet, something odd has happened over the last decade or so and somehow, at least in certain circles, *Be Here Now* has become the most talked about Oasis album. Part of that is based on the so-called narrative that has sprung up around Oasis. *Definitely Maybe* and *(What's The Story) Morning Glory?* are the well-known, hit-filled masterpieces, and starting with *Standing On The Shoulder Of Giants*, the albums become inconsistent, with *Don't Believe The Truth* and, to a lesser extent, *Dig Out Your Soul* bringing that consistency back. Fans and critics alike, on the other hand, struggle to define *Be Here Now*. Is it a misunderstood masterpiece, maybe even their best album? Is it a bloated mess of an album where every song goes on for at least a minute too long? Is it somewhere in between those two poles? Fans will continue to go back and forth and journalists will continue to argue both extremes. What is true is that there is a lot to be said about the album.

Like other albums of its ilk, *Be Here Now* is *a lot*. A lot of that is good, there are some great songs and Liam, especially, shines brightly while Noel proves, yet again, that he is a masterful songwriter. *Be Here Now* is a loud, dense and long album. Noel and the rest of the band were given free rein to make whatever album they wanted to make after the smashing success of *(What's The Story) Morning Glory?,* and the album that emerged is *Be Here Now*, a bloated masterpiece if ever there was one. As Chuck Klosterman points out in a piece he wrote for *Grantland*:

It's sometimes viewed as the record that killed Britpop. And people turned on Oasis when this happened. The bloated, bass-empty, blow-stretched songs validated critics who'd claimed their earlier work was overrated, and the absence of a ubiquitous single (such as 1995's 'Wonderwall') eroded their position in the culture. From a public opinion standpoint, they never truly recovered.

If saying they never truly recovered feels like an overstatement, Klosterman is right that *Be Here Now*, and more accurately, the aftermath, marked a major shift in how people viewed and talked about Oasis. They continued to score number-one albums and singles, but something changed. Few people in the world have a better perspective on this era in the band's history than Paolo Hewitt, who said:

> Over half a million people went out and bought *Be Here Now* on the first day of release. It was just craziness... I remember thinking after Knebworth ... you should have said, 'that's it', and then it would have gone down in history as just amazing. Instead, it just sort of slowly began to disintegrate.

The palpable excitement surrounding the release of *Be Here Now* is hard to appreciate more than 25 years removed from it. It became Britain's fastest-selling in history, not being beaten until Adele put out *25*. Further, a majority of the reviews were glowing, perhaps overly glowing, almost feeling like many critics reviewed it without really listening to it. They wanted to like it, they wanted to crown it as a masterpiece because of how big and culturally ubiquitous Oasis were. Despite their fame and fortune, the band were still, somewhat at least, everymen. They had woven themselves into the fabric of British culture, arguably to an extent not seen since The Beatles, and there was no option to not like them anymore. Coupled with this was the fact that several major publications gave lukewarm reviews of *(What's The Story) Morning Glory?* and they wanted to atone for that. Almost just as quickly, the pendulum started swinging the other way; it was now a disappointment, sales-wise, because it did not sell as many copies as the previous record. The second and third wave of reviews were not nearly as glowing, and then Noel started to disown the record. Songs from *Be Here Now* were largely absent from Oasis setlists for all the tours after the actual *Be Here Now* tour, and no songs from the album appeared on the *Stop The Clocks* compilation. Interestingly, Oasis did play two songs from *Be Here Now* at their 1996 Knebworth concert, a full year before the album would be released. Noel's continuous disparaging comments aside, the dust has settled around the album, even with a 2016 deluxe box-set release of *Be Here Now*, and the album has gained 'or re-gained' something of a cult-like status amongst certain fans. It's now easier to find retrospective articles on *Be Here Now* than it is *Definitely Maybe*. Jeff Slate wrote in *Rock Cellar Magazine*:

In the end, *Be Here Now* was the beginning of the end of the classic lineup of Oasis. When the band returned with 2000's *Standing On The Shoulder Of Giants*, both Bonehead and Guigsy were gone and the sound was remarkably different. *Be Here Now*, therefore, marked the end of a glorious era of 90s music that holds many memories, good, bad and mixed, for those who were part of those times.

And so here they are, 12 flawed, at times brilliant, usually overly long songs that make up a major part of the Oasis legacy.

'D'You Know What I Mean?' (N. Gallagher)

A-side single. Released: 7 July 1997. UK: 1

As with their first two albums, *Be Here Now* arrives in remarkable fashion. 'D'You Know What I Mean?' represents everything that worked brilliantly on *Be Here Now* and is the sound of a band on top of the world. This song *had* to be larger than life, as that is what the expectation was at the time. It opens with the sound of an aircraft that was recorded on an airstrip next to the house that Noel was renting while writing *Be Here Now*. The song opens up slowly with plenty of feedback, samples and vocal effects dominating. Liam enters at 1:07 with 'step off the train all alone at dawn', and what follows are two verses of classic Noel-isms, with a couple of Beatles references and a Dylan nod tossed in for good measure. The song simply feels massive and Liam's delivery is spot-on. It's hard to read the lyrics and not see it as Noel's way of saying that they, Oasis, are on the summit and are the future:

The sun in the sky never raised an eye to me
The blood on the trax and must be mine
The fool on the hill and I feel fine
Don't look back cos you know what you might see.

The chorus is the most famous part of the song, for simply posing the title of the song as a question:

All my people right here, right now
D'you know what I mean? Yeah, yeah

Ironically, Noel has said he was trying to make a profound statement in the chorus, but simply could not come up with anything that fit. Other lines, such as, 'Coming in a mess, going out in style', refer to this band of young men from Manchester who were now driving fancy cars and doing expensive drugs. Famously, the track is layered with guitars upon guitars and certainly sounds like the most produced song in their catalogue up until this point, even including Morse code in the background. This was, of course, the same band that made *Definitely Maybe*, but it was also clearly a different band.

The accompanying music video is almost as big as the song itself, with significantly larger production values than previous Oasis videos. Taking place in something of a post-apocalyptic world, with helicopters flying all around, the video was a marked departure from older music videos the band had produced. Something of a studio gem, with many of the effects heard on the song difficult to reproduce in a live setting, the song has not been played live since 2002. Always appearing high on lists of greatest Oasis songs, this is a clear highlight of *Be Here Now* and a canonical Oasis song.

'My Big Mouth' (N. Gallagher)
British guitar music was what Oasis did best and they mastered the formula on their first two albums and associated singles. And, really, besides the opening track, *Be Here Now* is a continuation of that same sound. This is not necessarily a bad thing, but it was in contrast to what some compatriots were doing, namely Radiohead, Blur, The Verve and Pulp, who all had either recently released albums that demonstrated a marked change in sound or were about to. These albums were all massive critical successes and their stature has not diminished over time, each one enjoying a level of acclaim that Oasis would never experience again, although *Don't Believe The Truth* came close. Oasis were more popular at their peak than any of those aforementioned bands and simply did not feel a need, nor did they have a collective desire to reinvent their sound. When they did make their biggest artistic leap with *Standing On The Shoulder Of Giants,* the results were mixed at best, at least in the eyes of the critics. So, *Be Here Now*, in some ways, winds up being the sound of a band being stuck and then coming down from the incredible heights, creatively of 1994-1995, and commercially of 1996. A song like 'My Big Mouth' certainly was not bad, but it was also part of an overall drop in batting average, song-wise, that pervaded the album.

It is one of the most aggressive songs in the Oasis catalogue, perhaps only second to 'Morning Glory' in terms of getting people pumped up at a gig. It's not aggressive in a punk-rock way, but because of the relentless layers of guitars and a sneering vocal from Liam. Some sources cite the number of guitars on this track alone at 26, with some other songs as high as 32 guitars. The pre-chorus is one of the most glorious things on the album and is incredibly catchy. The chorus itself talks about walking slowly down the hall of fame. Around this time, Noel was beginning to write more self-referential lyrics, and the second verse opens up with:

I ain't never spoke to God
And I ain't never been to heaven
But you assumed I knew the way
Even though the map was given

1996, the year all the songs were written and recorded, saw Liam and Noel gaining new levels of fame and cultural cache; Noel, especially, was being viewed as something of a guru, which he felt was hogwash. Lyrically, Noel would cite this notion as inspiration for this song, specifically the way in which fans would assume that rock stars 'knew the way'. These lyrics are very similar to those found in the Emily Dickinson poem, 'I Never Spoke With God'.

Like most of the songs on *Be Here Now*, the song overstays its welcome, but for the first half at least, it's a damn fun rocker. One of the few songs on *Be Here Now* that has had something of a live career, it was brought back into the fold fairly regularly in 2009 for the *Dig Out Your Soul* tour.

'Magic Pie' (N. Gallagher)

Be Here Now was the first album in which the tracks were fully recorded before Liam *then* came in to record his vocals. The band were not often in the studio together and it led to a slightly more disjointed sound. On tracks like 'Magic Pie', Liam's involvement was nothing. Slowly, but consistently, Noel would start to take more lead vocals on both album tracks and especially B-sides. On *Be Here Now,* he recorded just one lead vocal and it was on this seven-minute, Mellotron-heavy mini-epic that winds up being one of the more forgettable songs on the album. Some interesting guitar work and interesting lyrics are balanced out by some of the weakest lyrics Noel ever penned, and a song length that is not justified by the product.

The opening couplet of the song was inspired by Liam when he asked Noel why he (Noel) never gets into any of the trouble that he (Liam) gets into.

An extraordinary guy
Can never have an ordinary day

Another part of the song was inspired by Tony Blair's speech at the Labour Party conference in the fall of 1996: 'there are but a thousand days preparing for a thousand years'. Noel Gallagher became friendly with Tony Blair after attending a Downing Street party in 1997 in the aftermath of a major Labour landslide victory in the general election that year. At the Brit Awards in 1996, Noel said that Blair was 'giving a little hope to the young people in this country'.

'Stand By Me' (N. Gallagher)

A-side single. Released: 22 September 1997. UK: 2

The second single released from *Be Here Now* and one that likely would have hit number one had it not been for Elton John's tribute to Princess Diana: his reworking of 'Candle In The Wind'. The previous two singles had gone right to number one, as would the next two. While not as anthemic as 'D'You Know What I Mean?', this is still a great mid-tempo ballad, exactly the type of song that Noel specialised in. Noel says he wrote this song while suffering food poisoning after attempting to cook a Sunday roast when he first moved to London, eventually reverting back to noodles.

Made a meal and threw it up on Sunday
I've got a lot of things to learn

The song as a whole has been interpreted differently by fans and critics but has remained one of the most acclaimed on the record. Some feel that Noel is talking about growing up and some attribute many of the lyrics to being about a one-sided relationship. Some lines at the end even put Noel in some hot water with Meg Matthews:

There is one thing I can never give you
My heart will never be your home

'That's about the private space you have – the place where I go to write my stuff. Meg was fairly upset by that', Noel would comment. 'Stand By Me' was the only song from *Be Here Now* to appear on the live album *Familiar To Millions,* and after being dropped in the Oasis setlists, it has been consistently played by Noel Gallagher in various solo incarnations. Liam Gallagher has also performed the song as a solo artist, and his reading of the song, which was eventually released on *MTV Unplugged (Live at Hull City Hall),* is one of the most effective versions ever performed. The night before the release of *Be Here Now* in 1997, there was a documentary about Oasis on BBC One, which was likely aired to capitalise on the excitement surrounding the album. During this broadcast, an acoustic version of the song is played, which many people regard as the ultimate version of the song. A terrific track from this era that likely should have been even more popular than it was. After all, as Noel described the song: 'It's a bit like 'Live Forever', I suppose, with a touch of 'All The Young Dudes' in the background – though I made sure I changed the chords'.

'I Hope, I Think, I Know' (N. Gallagher)
For some fans, this is the highlight of *Be Here Now* and should have been a live staple, perhaps even a single. An underrated gem of a song, this is one of the poppiest songs in their catalogue, contrasting nicely with the other songs on the album. It's a jubilant blast of pop candy sounding, at times, like the cousin of 'Step Out'. In fact, Noel felt it was *too* pop and said as much to *Q Magazine* when doing a track-by-track breakdown of the album: 'The only reason it's on the album is for balance because it's quite fast. I liked the demo, but it's too pop for me now. I'm slowing down. I'm getting into my voodoo stage'.

Noel was further dismissive of the tune, suggesting it would be the song from the album that no one mentions, and even if that suggestion has not totally held up, the tune is surprisingly overlooked on best-of lists, concert setlists, etc. At 4:22, this is one of the songs on *Be Here Now* that feels like it's perfectly timed and, in fact, maybe even ends too soon.

One theory on the meaning of the lyrics purports that they deal with the paparazzi hounding Noel. 1996 was an especially brutal year for the paparazzi and the Gallagher brothers, eventually getting to a point where the gossip was being talked about more than the music for a period of time. Another theory is that Noel is making veiled references about being sick of critics and fans comparing Oasis to older bands. A very worthy addition to any weekend playlist.

'The Girl In The Dirty Shirt' (N. Gallagher)
At 5:49, we are back in the territory of a song that overstays its welcome, which is a shame, as this song is a pleasant one with some interesting musical and lyrical bits going on. The chord structure, according to Noel, came straight from 'Cry Baby Cry' by The Beatles, although it's not an obvious call-back by any means. Noel and Liam sing some call-and-response vocals, which are always a hit and seemingly always work well. The titular girl in the dirty shirt is Meg Matthews; Noel saw her at a gig in 1994 ironing a dirty shirt, as she had not brought enough clean clothes along with her. It's hard to describe the track as filler, yet it is certainly one of the more forgotten tracks on the album.

'Fade In-Out' (N. Gallagher)
The song which has provided casual fans with the answer to the trivia question: on which Oasis track does Johnny Depp contribute slide guitar? Now, astute fans will point out that Johnny Depp also played guitar on the Warchild Version of 'Fade Away', with none other than Kate Moss playing a tambourine on that same track. Nevertheless, it still comes as a surprise to some that Johnny Depp is featured in the *Be Here Now* liner notes. Depp and Moss were friends with Noel and remained as such after the couple's breakup in 1997. The most oft-told version of the story of how Depp wound up on the album is simply that Noel was too drunk to play guitar. Luckily, Depp was hanging around in the Caribbean for the party atmosphere and abundance of drugs. Being an adept guitar player, he was able to contribute the notable slide guitar sections, which give the song a lot of its unique flavour. Noel commented on how grateful he was to have Depp around:

> But I'm glad it happened. If he hadn't been around, we would have had to get some fat old geezer who'd be telling us about how he played with Clapton in 76 and did a slide solo that lasted four fucking months.

Featuring what can only be described as a Western vibe, 'Fade In-Out', at nearly seven minutes in length, is one of the few songs on the album that,

Above: The version of Oasis responsible for most of their biggest hits. The 'jacket look' would be immortalised by the brothers. (*Alamy*)

Left: The cover of 'Supersonic', the first Oasis single. Everyone but Liam almost looks like a wax figurine. The first microdot cover, of which there would be many more. (*Creation Records*)

Right: The 'Live Forever' cover. The house, 251 Menlove Avenue, is where John Lennon grew up and is one of the earliest Beatles references found in the Oasis universe. (*Creation Records*)

Right: Their debut album *Definitely Maybe* marks the fourth official Oasis release. The cover has been parodied over the years, perhaps a sign of its popularity. Notice the prominence of Burt Bacharach. (*Creation Records*)

Left: The third best-selling studio album of all time in the UK, (*What's The Story*) *Morning Glory?* is a monster of an album. Sleeve designer Brian Cannon has his back to the camera and DJ Sean Rowley is walking towards the listener. (*Creation Records*)

Left: Inspired by Belgian surrealist Rene Magritte, the 'Wonderwall' single contains, what is to many, the ultimate Oasis B-side: 'The Masterplan'. As for 'Wonderwall' itself, it is the most-streamed song of the 1990s on Spotify. (*Creation Records*)

Right: The hot streak of singles continues with 'Don't Look Back In Anger'. The Beatles-inspired sleeve refers to when Ringo left the band for a few weeks and returned to flowers around a drum kit. (*Creation Records*)

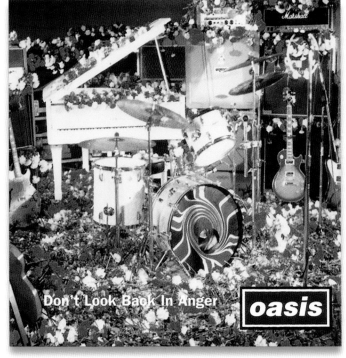

Right: Their longest and, in many ways, most controversial album, *Be Here Now* continues to elicit debates amongst fans and journalists. The cover, a hodgepodge of BBC props, even spurred a little legal controversy. (*Creation Records*)

Left: As the second single released from *Be Here Now*, 'Stand By Me' peaked at number two. The single contains the gem of a B-side 'Going Nowhere'. (*Creation Records*)

Left: Liam, with his God-given cool, once said about himself: 'I am the most spiritual person in the world. I have feelings no one else has'.

Right: 'We're not arrogant; we just believe we're the best band in the world'. Maybe Noel was right, at least for a year or two.

Left: Never released as a single in the UK, 'Morning Glory' is cited by most fans as one of their favourite tracks.

Right: Paul McGuigan, or Guigsy, was always overshadowed by the Gallagher brothers during his time in Oasis. Even in this still from the 'Morning Glory' video, he sits in the shadow of Liam.

Left: If Liam is to be believed, he cried during the recording of 'Don't Go Away'. Here in the music video, he delivers a terrific vocal performance.

Right: In this still from the 'Don't Go Away' video, Liam looks as pensive as he ever would.

Left: *The Masterplan* collected many of the best Oasis B-sides from the first three albums and is often referred to as the third-best Oasis album. (*Creation Records*)

Right: The difficult album in the catalogue, at least for some, *Standing On The Shoulder Of Giants* saw Oasis stretching out sonically in a way that was largely absent on the first three albums. (*Big Brother*)

Left: 'Who Feels Love?' is the most obvious example of the psychedelic/Eastern sound on *Standing On The Shoulder Of Giants*. Paul Weller would record a version of the B-side 'One Way Road'. (*Big Brother*)

Right: Available in six different formats for the hardcore fan, *Familiar To Millions* may not be essential, but the version of 'Gas Panic!' contained herein makes it almost worth the price of admission alone. (*Big Brother*)

Left: Despite Liam citing it as his least favourite Oasis record, *Heathen Chemistry* proved that Noel was still capable of writing killer singles. (*Big Brother*)

Right: Their sixth UK number-one single, '**The Hindu Times**' received overwhelmingly positive reviews from critics. Noel's beautiful 'Idler's Dream' is tucked away as a B-side. (*Big Brother*)

Left: Garnering their best reviews since (*What's The Story*) *Morning Glory?*, their sixth album *Don't Believe The Truth* was seen as a return to form and contained some of Noel's most effective songs. (*Big Brother*)

Right: Cited by *Q Magazine* as the greatest track of 2005, 'The Importance Of Being Idle' is a highlight of latter-era Oasis singles. (*Big Brother*)

Left: How do you make a successful Oasis compilation? Call it a 'best of', *not* a greatest hits and let Noel pick a dream setlist of sorts. *Stop The Clocks*, despite some legitimate gripes, works very well. (*Big Brother*)

Right: The seventh and final studio album from Oasis. *Dig Out Your Soul* may have been front-loaded, but was a respectable ending to a great studio catalogue. (*Big Brother*)

Left: The first lead single since 'Supersonic' to fail to reach number one in the UK. Despite that, 'The Shock Of The Lightning' was, for many, the highlight of their last album. (*Big Brother*)

Right: *Time Flies…1994-2009*, which collects every UK single, does not work as well as it should. The out-of-order track listing does not help at all. (*Big Brother*)

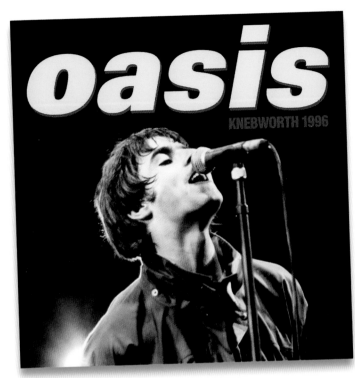

Left: While Maine Road purists will disagree, for many, *Knebworth 1996* was the highlight of their career. (*Big Brother*)

Above: The brothers were in their element at Knebworth in 1996. Liam, tambourine in hand, was hard to beat when he was on, and he was certainly on for this performance.

Above: 'Sure, Noel is good. But I'm better'. Never one for being humble, Liam was always good for a headline. (*Simon Ritter*)

Below: Liam's iconic stance has become one of the famous parts of his legacy, with dolls for sale that mimic his stance and microphone positioning.

Above: As it stands as of this writing, Bonehead and Liam are the only two Oasis members confirmed for the *Definitely Maybe* anniversary tour in 2024. (*Matthias Nareyek*)

Below: Over the years, too much ink has been spilt about the Blur vs Oasis feud. Here they are, post-feud, two of the most talented songwriters of their generation. (*Dave M. Benett*)

Above: 'I love the Beatles. What more can I say? I'm not gonna lie to you. I love 'em. They make me happy. And I think they were the best, and still are', as said by Liam, pictured here with a friend. (*Dave J. Hogan*)

Below: Noel famously attended a Downing Street party in 1997 after having praised Tony Blair at the Brit Awards for 'giving a little hope to young people in this country'. (*Rebecca Naden*)

oasis

DON'T STOP... (DEMO)

Left: At the time of its release in April 2020, 'Don't Stop…' was the first new Oasis music in 11 years. A fine latter-day effort. (*Big Brother*)

Right: Released in 2016, *Oasis: Supersonic* is a great documentary and consists largely of the Gallagher brothers speaking – you can't beat it. (*Mat Whitecross*)

A MAT WHITECROSS FILM

SUPERSONIC

IN CINEMAS THIS OCTOBER

despite its length, doesn't leave you wishing it would end just a minute sooner. Towards the end of the song, Noel also works the sound of him screaming onto the track; what he said was the very last sound recorded for the song. Working equally well as a live track, Oasis played the song regularly in 1997.

'Don't Go Away' (N. Gallagher)
Released as a single in Japan 'and now a collector's item', but oddly never in the UK, this is the track on the album that should have been a bigger hit, sounding more radio-ready than 'Stand By Me' was. Along with 'All Around The World', it is one of the oldest tracks on the album, with a demo version from Japan in 1994 being included on the *Be Here Now* box set and Tony McCarrol saying it was part of the 1993 session with The Real People.

This is a song about losing someone close, or rather not wanting to lose someone close, specifically about Noel's mum. Opening with prominent lead guitar work by Noel, and featuring an excellent Liam vocal performance and Bacharach-esque horns, this had all the markings of a hit. On an interesting side note, the song is analysed by British philosopher Roger Scruton in his book 'Modern Culture'. The lyrics that he chooses to focus on are:

Damn my education, I can't find the words to say
About the things caught in my mind

Scruton's analysis is worth looking up and while arguably an over-analysis, it lends some gravitas to a band that wasn't used to it. The song also features very 'Champagne Supernova'-esque guitar work as the song enters its middle-eight, right around 2:32. 'Don't Go Away' was one of the highlights of the *Be Here Now* tour but wasn't touched much live after that. Noel, however, has played the song very frequently, including on *The Dreams We Have As Children*.

The Japan-only single release is something of a collector's item amongst fans, always one of the priciest singles to buy online. Featuring a live version of 'Cigarettes & Alcohol', 'Sad Song' and the Warchild version of 'Fade Away', it is certainly one of the more interesting singles.

'Be Here Now' (N. Gallagher)
Ironically, given it is the title track, 'Be Here Now' tends to fly under the radar on the album of the same name. It was not released as a single, it was not a proper hit, but it is still something of a fan favourite and a rocking, goofy song that does not drag as many other songs on the album do. It's a very straightforward song with a consistent pounding rhythm permeating the entire track, and a guitar solo tossed in for good measure. Some listeners have even compared the song to a train, with its constant pounding, forward motion. It is notable, lyrically, for some references to

Digsy's – 'Digsy's Diner', of course, being the name of an Oasis song – and the line about singing a song from 'Let It Be', because why not toss a Beatles reference in for good measure?

In terms of where the title itself comes from, another Beatles reference rears its head in the form of George Harrison's song of the same name. There is also a quote attributed to John Lennon, but difficult to verify, in which he says the purpose of rock 'n' roll is to 'be here now'. Ram Dass, an American spiritual guru, also published a book in 1971 titled *Be Here Now*, which may have passed through Noel's hands at some point. The song was a setlist mainstay on the *Be Here Now* tour and has shown up in Liam's setlists over the years as well. For all the attention that other songs on the album receive, this one probably deserves a little more.

'All Around the World' (N. Gallagher)
A-side single. Released: 12 January 1998. UK: 1

For detractors of *Be Here Now*, this song represents everything that was wrong with the album, becoming synonymous with over-indulgence and ridiculous song lengths. Not only is it the longest Oasis song, but it is also the longest song to ever hit the number-one spot in the UK. More string-laden and epic than even 'Whatever', this is Oasis at their most extravagant, their 'Hey Jude' and 'All You Need Is Love' rolled into one, to force a Beatles reference.

Despite being the type of song that a band would usually not write or record early in their career, simply due to the logistics of including and paying for an orchestra, this is one of the first songs that Noel ever wrote. There is excellent footage in the *Oasis: Supersonic* that shows the band rehearsing this. Noel wanted to wait until they had the production budget to do this song justice:

> I wrote this one ages ago, before 'Whatever'. It was 12 minutes long then. It was a matter of being able to afford to record it. But now we can get away with the 36-piece orchestra. And the longer, the better, as far as I'm concerned. If it's good. I can see what people are going to say but fuck 'em, basically.

At 9:20, the sheer length of the song is the first thing people usually talk about when referencing 'All Around The World'. It's a simple song, both musically and lyrically, but there is a lot going on and there are several distinct passages within the first part of the song, it just takes a long time to navigate between them. Starting out as a relatively straightforward pop song, the first 'na-na-na-na' comes at 2:44, and until the song ends at 9:20, the song is essentially in perpetual refrain mode with a few new phrases thrown in: 'it's gonna be okay' and 'and I know what I know'. For its length, it must be said that the song doesn't feel as long as others on *Be Here Now*. Oasis had the gall to play this live on the *Be Here Now* tour, but it was never touched again by the band after that, Noel having distanced himself from the album; 'All Around The World' is, in some ways, the most explicit representation of *Be Here Now*.

The last UK single to feature Bonehead and Guigsy, 'All Around The World' also represents something of a start of the second half of Oasis' career. The next time Oasis released a single, they were no longer the most popular band in the world. Their singles would not be as warmly received and Noel would start to enter a phase of relative inconsistency. When *Be Here Now* was released in August 1997, Oasis were still yet to record a plethora of their best songs, but their story was now going to be told in a different way.

'It's Getting Better (Man!!)' (N. Gallagher)
The unenviable task of following 'All Around The World' fell to this track, which has flown under the radar ever since *Be Here Now* was released. A sleazier song than Oasis typically played, this was, in Noel's estimation, more of a Stones song than a Beatles song:

> I wrote this jamming on stage with the band in America. A really happy tune, even though there was a load of bad shit going down. Because we get connected with The Beatles all the time, I thought I'd write a Rolling Stones song. You can almost see Keith and Ronnie with fags in their mouths, giving it some.

The song could have easily ended at the 4:41 mark and, in my opinion, would have likely been more fondly remembered. The outro of the song, essentially the last 2:20, features the title being repeated 33 times: 'thanks, Richard Bowes'. As such, it feels like another over-indulgent track that could have greatly benefited from some objective quality control and trimming. Played live in 1996 and then throughout the *Be Here Now* tour, this forgotten track is worthy but also emblematic of everything that did not work on the album.

'All Around The World (Reprise)' (N. Gallagher)
A strings and backwards guitar-soaked reprise of their most epic song closes their most epic album. The feet clumping at the end, walking towards the door, belong to Brian Cannon, who was the sleeve designer for the album. The final sound, of course, is that of a door slamming, the symbolism of which cannot be overstated: the official end of Oasis Mark I.

Be Here Now B-Sides/EPs
'Stay Young' (N. Gallagher)
B-side of 'D'You Know What I Mean?'
The *Be Here Now* B-sides show a marked drop in overall quality from the treasure trove of riches that were the *(What's The Story) Morning Glory?*

B-sides. This is not to say they are bad songs, as any batch that includes 'Stay Young' and 'Going Nowhere' cannot be called lacking, they are just not uniformly excellent. 'Stay Young' is the most famous B-side from *Be Here Now*, the chorus acting as a calling card for Oasis fans everywhere:

> Hey, stay young and invincible
> 'Cause we know just what we are
> And come what may we're unstoppable
> 'Cause we know what we are

One of two singles from this era included on *The Masterplan* compilation, this is one of the poppiest songs from the era and was certainly more radio-friendly than its A-side. Noel has stated that he is not the biggest fan of the song, feeling it sounds too Britpop. He expanded upon his feelings in an interview with *Melody Maker* after *Be Here Now* was released:

> I don't like it. I wrote it by mistake for the last album. Why it didn't go on the album is because, when I got back to England, I wrote 'Magic Pie'. Sounds like The Kinks as well, I think. I don't like the guitar solo on it. I don't like the sound of it either...

I imagine most fans would have preferred 'Stay Young' over 'Magic Pie' on *Be Here Now*, as it would have lent more of a classic Oasis sound to the record. Only played by Oasis in 1997, this would have been a great track to drop into subsequent setlists, with Noel also playing it as a solo acoustic track a few times around the time of *Be Here Now*. An anthem for the youth, an anthem for the fans.

'Angel Child (Demo)' (N. Gallagher)
B-side of 'D'You Know What I Mean?'
Recorded during the Mustique sessions, this is another minor-key Noel ballad that always made for a great B-side. It's a fine song, much like 'If We Shadows', but it just kind of lingers, feeling like a demo that Noel never returned to, which is exactly what it was – until briefly resurrected by Noel for a couple of solo gigs in 2012. Lyrically, the song would hit on themes that Noel would further explore during the *Standing On The Shoulder Of Giants* era:

> Cos I gave all my money to people and things
> And the price I'm still paying for the shit that it brings
> Doesn't fill me with the hope for the songs that you sing

Some have speculated that the song was written for Noel's daughter and served as a warning for her not to get caught up in some of the things that he did. Either way, it works well as a demo and is something fans can hope that Noel pulls out of his hat again.

'Heroes' (D. Bowie, B. Eno)
B-side of 'D'You Know What I Mean?'
What is perhaps David Bowie's greatest song is a fairly odd choice for an Oasis B-side. On the other hand, as Richard Bowes points out: '...The direct romance of the lyrics correlates well with Noel's general mindset. 'We could be heroes' is the basic message that informs everything the man writes'.

The song manages to impressively reproduce the iconic swirling guitar of the original but, of course, cannot totally reproduce the production of the original masterpiece. Noel, on lead vocal, starts at a totally different point in the song than Bowie does, Noel beginning with 'I wish I could swim' as opposed to 'I, I will be king'. His vocal delivery rhythmically contrasts with Bowie's original but stays pretty faithful to the song where it matters, even reproducing the excellent background vocals: 'I remember', 'by the wall', 'over our heads', 'nothing could fall'. Noel says this was the first David Bowie song that he heard and that the song and seeing Bowie live changed his life, this remaining his favourite song by Bowie: 'The sentiment is amazing: We can be heroes, if only for one day. We all can't make it in life, but we can feel like we can make it, for one day at a time. That's why it's my favourite'.

As with 'Strawberry Fields Forever', 'Heroes' found its way into Noel's acoustic sets, where it was often performed in an even more enjoyable way than the version presented here. Wrapping up what was a relatively confounding single, it's another one that did not appear on the *Be Here Now* deluxe reissue, likely due to some sort of copyright issue.

'(I Got) The Fever' (N. Gallagher)
B-side of 'Stand By Me'
This is the type of song that Noel could write in his sleep, and maybe even did. Relatively catchy and straightforward, this has a huge chorus and is perhaps Alan White's shining moment on record; Alan White always flew under the radar as a member of Oasis, as most non-Gallagher members did. Wisely, Noel let Liam sing this one, and while the lyrics don't say much of importance, we do get a 'I can feel it comin' in the air tonight' line. Not dissimilar to 'My Big Mouth' or 'Stay Young', both of which work better, this was a wise choice to bury as a B-side.

'My Sister Lover' (N. Gallagher)
B-side of 'Stand By Me'
This is a song that is less famous for the content or quality of the song itself but because of the story behind it. Oasis used to practise in the same Manchester rehearsal space as a group called Sister Lover. It is that same band who essentially invited Oasis to play the infamous King Tut show

in Glasgow. Alan McGhee was there and was intrigued enough to start the process of offering Oasis a record deal. This is, of course, a shortened version of the legend. This song also forms something of a trilogy with two other songs. The original demo of 'Lock All The Doors' is essentially 'My Sister Lover' in its infant form. Fast Forward to 2015, and Noel Gallagher's High Flying Birds released 'Lock All The Doors' on their *Chasing Yesterday* album.

The lyrics are an early example of Noel writing disparagingly about religion:

> Faith in the lord is something I can never have
> Faith in my sister is gonna set me free
> Faith in the lord is something I will never have
> 'Cause the lord I know don't got no faith in me

The lyrics also provide some low-hanging fruit for fans to accuse the song's narrator of fantasising about his sister, with the refrain, 'my love, I'm your brother'. Prominent piano chords populate the song and it moves along in a relatively pleasant way but goes on too long – 'what else is new?' – and was better left to B-side status. Allegedly removed from *The Masterplan* in favour of 'Going Nowhere', which was the right call, this is one of the more under-the-radar B-sides from the first three albums.

'Going Nowhere' (N. Gallagher)
B-side of 'Stand By Me'
Sounding more like a Burt Bacharach tune than any other song in the Oasis catalogue, this is a highlight of the 'Stand By Me' single, thankfully and justifiably included on *The Masterplan,* where most people likely initially heard it, including this author. Noel was at his peak as a writer when he was imagining where he wanted to go and how he wanted to get there. His aspiration songs are some of his best. Noel wrote this song shortly after signing their first record deal, and as an early Noel song, this fits squarely into that category.

> I'm gonna get me a motor car
> Maybe a Jaguar maybe a plan or a day of fame
> I'm gonna be a millionaire so can you take me there
> Want to be wild 'cause my life's so tame

Nick Ingman, who arranged the strings for many Oasis songs, would say that Noel was almost as equally into Bacharach as he was into The Beatles. The strings on 'Going Nowhere' are perfectly placed and Ingman is masterful here. 'Don't Go Away' carried that Bacharachian stamp as well; however, this is Noel's most successful Bacharach-esque composition.

'The Fame' (N. Gallagher)
B-side of 'All Around The World'

1998 and 1999 would be very quiet years in terms of new Oasis releases, with the 'All Around The World' single being the only new music Oasis would release until 2000. 'All Around The World' is perhaps the forgotten single of the *Be Here Now* era, as none of these singles were selected for inclusion on *The Masterplan* compilation, which is a shame, as the batting average here is pretty damn high. Leading off with 'The Fame', which forms something of a trio with 'Step Out' and 'I Hope I Think I Know', it is a supremely catchy pop song, feeling slightly out of place with most songs from the era. Noel takes lead vocals on both original B-sides on the single, and this is another one that would have likely benefited had Liam been on lead vocals. The easy reading here is that this is a song about fame, hangers-on and people waiting for you to fail. As Noel would relay to *NME* in 1997:

> I can't get that angry about fame, though, because when I was on the dole, there was nothing I liked more than seeing a celebrity being put through the fucking mill, you know. We get paid enough money to do what we do and if that's the price, a little snidey story here and there, then so be it.

Never performed live and never appearing on any compilations, this is a B-side that is forgotten by all but the fans. A shame, too.

'Flashbax' *(N. Gallagher)*
B-side of 'All Around The World'

Another Noel-sung B-side, this one is in his classic mid-tempo rocker vein with a cheerful and loud chorus. The verses do not work quite as well and would be indicative of the types of tunes that would populate *Standing On The Shoulder Of Giants*. Most notably, at about 3:14, we get a whistling breakdown replete with a slew of cymbals crashing. The song title can be taken literally, with flashbacks and visions of childhood being the theme of the track's story. The weaker of the two original B-sides featured on 'All Around The World', it is still worth hearing.

'Street Fighting Man' (M. Jagger, K. Richards)
B-side of 'All Around The World'

Continuing the trend of covering classic rock tunes, this is another slam dunk for Liam and the band. With lyrics seemingly written just for Liam and a back-to-basics music approach, this cover works on every level. Taking an electric approach to the guitar work, as opposed to the layered acoustic guitars of the original, this version otherwise stays relatively faithful to the 1968 version that was one of the best Rolling Stones songs of the era.

The Rolling Stones and Oasis were tangentially related, especially during the *Be Here Now* era. The Mustique Demos were laid down at Mick Jagger's residence in Mustique. The song that would become 'Be Here Now' was originally demoed as 'Trip Inside', which featured Noel using a piano found at Mick's residence. As the story goes, the toy piano essentially just played samples of the Stones' song 'Honky Tonk Women'. When the *Be Here Now* deluxe reissue came out in 2016, the original demo was released on some early pressings and on iTunes on the first day, yet was almost instantly pulled due to copyright concerns. Most pressings of the deluxe version of *Be Here Now* feature an instrumental for the track titled 'Trip Inside'. Beyond that, on 'It's Getting Better (Man!!)', Noel was purposely going for a Stones vibe, even if the end result is equal parts 80s hard rock. And, who can forget when Keith Richards labelled Oasis 'crap' before saying: 'these guys are just obnoxious. Grow up and then come back and see if you can hang'.

So, was this cover released ironically? It was recorded after Keith made his comments. Either way, a darn good cover with Liam, especially, doing exactly what he does best. Sadly, this is not to be found on the *Be Here Now* deluxe reissue, likely due to copyright or simply not wanting to pay Mick and Keith any royalties.

The songs on *Be Here Now* are notably devoid of bass guitar, with the three B-sides collected here, especially 'Street Fighting Man', being relatively bass-prominent. Paul McGuigan, aka Quigsy, was never going to fool anyone into thinking he was the greatest bass player ever, but he had a great, workmanlike sound that was integral to the heyday of Oasis. He quit the band in 1999, within weeks of Bonehead departing, and, if you believe Noel, he quit via fax and the pair never spoke again. In the months before he left, Oasis were in the South of France and engaged in very un-fun sessions for the soon-to-be fourth album, but for Guigsy, the decision to eventually quit came earlier. He was an introvert who loved smoking pot and didn't like the heights that the band had scaled – it simply was not fun anymore. His sister Mary says, as quoted in 'Some Might Say' by Richard Bowes:

It's weird that Paul was quite shy and introverted, yet was in what is seen as one of the biggest bands that the world has ever seen. That seems a bit weird, but he was always at the back and kind of anonymous. He didn't like fame, didn't like the attention. He's just not that kind of person. I cannot believe, to this day, that he ever got up on stage. Any stage, even in a pub.

As the guitar fades and 'Street Fighting Man' ends, fans would not hear new Oasis music until February 2000. Noel and Liam would keep relatively busy making music with others, but the Oasis that would return would be a new band; new members, new sound, new attitude and never quite able to consistently capture what made them so special to so many people.

'If We Shadows (Demo)' (N. Gallagher)

Noel at his most introspective, this is another minor-key ballad that he always excelled at, in the vein of the 'Angel Child' demo. This song was relatively unheard of until the 2016 deluxe reissue of the album, where it appeared on the second disc alongside a host of other interesting songs and demos. It certainly would not have fit on *Be Here Now*, but could have made an excellent B-side, not unlike something such as 'Sad Song' or the Noel ballads that would show up on the next half-dozen or so singles. These are perhaps the most interesting lyrics, perhaps a rare instance of Noel showing solidarity with Liam:

There are things calling my mind
Nobody knows what's wrong
To me and my brother

Perhaps it was too soul-bearing to be released, or perhaps Noel simply could not find a place for it. Either way, it was a welcome addition to the reissue box set.

'Setting Sun (Live Radio Broadcast)' (N. Gallagher)

One of the most acclaimed and popular songs that Noel Gallagher has been involved with is the 1996 Chemical Brothers masterpiece 'Setting Sun'. The version included here on the *Be Here Now* box set is an acoustic version of the song performed solely by Noel. The reinterpreted 1996 dance song masterpiece took Noel's lyrics and voice and turned it into one of the most acclaimed songs of the 1990s. 'Setting Sun' itself is essentially just a reworked version of the early Oasis track 'Comin' On Strong'. The version presented here is similar in style and sound to other acoustic ballads at the time that Noel was singing. Oasis took some flack in the wake of *Be Here Now*, amongst many other things directly related to that album, for not being as forward-thinking as their other contemporaries. Noel was not flexing his interests as much as he perhaps wanted to. Oasis would become a little more experimental with *Standing On The Shoulder Of Giants*, but they were never pushing the envelope and evolving in a way that, say, Blur was. Noel, to his credit, knew which way the wind was blowing and his collaboration with The Chemical Brothers is a testament to that.

Working with The Chemical Brothers and meeting people in the dance field has opened my eyes to loads of different ways of working. We limit ourselves because of... rock 'n' roll. If you can't produce it live, then it isn't worth doing? Fuck that shit! If you can't produce it live, then find a way of doing it. Push yourself. That's the way it's going to go with us, with a bit of luck.

Noel may have over-promised a little with his intention of being more experimental going forward, but his heart was at least in the right place.

As heard on *Be Here Now*, the intro to 'D'You Know What I Mean?', and the song in general, was notably sample-heavy and was likely emblematic of the direction that Noel wanted to go in. Additionally, Noel created a remix version of the Beck song 'Devil's Haircut' that further demonstrated his interest in creating new sounds and exploring new directions.

'Untitled' (N. Gallagher)
Yet another minor-chord ballad, this is very similar to 'If We Shadows', so similar, in fact, that it's no wonder they were kept in the vault until the deluxe reissue in 2016. Sometimes referred to as 'The One I'll Never Know' because of the lyrics, this is another enjoyable solo Gallagher tune, albeit forgettable in that it's hard to distinguish from several other tunes of the era.

'Help! (Live In L.A.)' (Lennon, McCartney)
Recorded live in 1998, this is a slowed-down, acoustic version of the famous Beatles track, with Noel being the only member of the band who appears on it. Noel wisely chose to slow the tempo down and handle it acoustically, as any full-band version would have inevitably been a let-down, given the complex harmonies and cultural reverence for the song. Noel sounds as if he's at his most vulnerable and it is not hard to see him connecting deeply with Lennon's lyrics: '...my life has changed in oh so many ways, my independence seems to vanish in the haze'. For all the Oasis and Beatles comparisons, and all the love that Noel and Liam have for the most famous group of all time, the pressure of being compared to The Beatles started to wear on Noel:

> At the end of the cycle of *Morning Glory*, I was hailed as the greatest songwriter since Lennon and McCartney. Now, I know that I'm not, and I knew I wasn't then. But the perception of everybody since that period has been, 'What the fuck happened to this guy? Wasn't he supposed to be the next fucking Beatles?' I never said that I was the greatest thing since Lennon and McCartney... well, actually, I'm lying. I probably did say that once or twice in interviews.

Noel played this acoustically as part of a dozen or so Oasis shows in early 1998 before it was dropped from the setlist. A nice little gem on the *Be Here Now* reissue box set and one worth adding to an introspective Noel playlist.

The Masterplan (1998)

The token, half-joking answer to the question of 'what is the third best Oasis album?', this 1998 collection of B-sides is certainly the most common answer. Released about a year after *Be Here Now*, this collection was a revelation to some and a simple reminder to others about how good Oasis was and could be. The majority of songs collected here are from the period of *Definitely Maybe* and *(What's The Story) Morning Glory?* when Noel was writing ridiculously consistently good songs, faster than the regular studio releases could keep up with. As such, and famously, a majority of these amazing songs were dumped onto B-sides. The Oasis faithful, who had been buying all the singles since April 1994, had heard all of these songs. But for the fans who hadn't been buying the singles, especially in America, where they weren't as readily available, this album was a revelation. Ask almost any Oasis fan to rank their favourite Oasis B-sides, and almost every one of them shows up on this album.

Fans can quibble about what was left off that should have been put on, etc. And while the album works splendidly as is, fans may have a few legitimate gripes. The first three singles are totally ignored, somewhat understandably, yet 'D'Yer Wanna Be A Spaceman?' would have been a perfect addition and provided some levity. From the 'Wonderwall' single, it is almost unforgivable that 'Round Are Way' is left off, while 'The Swamp Song' is included. Noel has made comments in the past about not liking songs that are too jolly, once describing 'Stay Young' as just that. Perhaps he felt 'Round Are Way' was too happy. Moving forward to the 'Don't Look Back In Anger' single, it is understandable why 'Step Out' was left off, catchy though it may be. The *Be Here Now* era singles are sparingly drawn from, with only two inclusions from that era collected on *The Masterplan*.

Ironically, the greatness of this collection and how well it functions as an album also crystallises what, for some, the problem was with Oasis's meteoric rise to fame. Debates about the merits of *Be Here Now* aside, almost everybody will agree that Oasis peaked with their first two albums and the accompanying singles. It felt like Noel was writing a great song every day. Instead of keeping some of those in the can, so to speak, they were dropped onto the nine singles that were released before 'D'You Know What I Mean?'. In the short term, this meant a consistency of B-sides that had not been experienced since The Beatles, but it also meant that Noel was out of his best songs by the time of *Be Here Now*. He was also master and commander of Oasis to the extent that he had no one around him to check his power, which arguably contributed to some of the bloatedness of *Be Here Now*. Imagine if two or three of these B-sides had been saved for *Standing On The Shoulder Of Giants*, it could have changed the course of Oasis history. Alas, whilst questions of 'what if?' are always fun, it is a dangerous game. Collected here are some of the greatest songs that Noel ever wrote. Enjoy.

Standing On The Shoulder Of Giants (2000)

Personnel:
Liam Gallagher: vocals
Noel Gallagher: guitar, vocals, bass, keyboards
Alan White: drums, percussion
Guest musicians:
Paul Stacey: keyboards, additional lead guitar on 'Fuckin' In The Bushes', backwards guitar on 'Who Feels Love?', bass on 'Who Feels Love?', 'Gas Panic!', 'I Can See A Liar' and 'Roll it Over', additional acoustic guitar on 'Where Did It All Go Wrong?', guitar solo on 'Roll It Over'
P.P. Arnold: backing vocals on 'Fuckin' In The Bushes', 'Put Yer Money Where Your Mouth Is' and 'Roll It Over'
Linda Lewis: backing vocals on 'Fuckin' In The Bushes', 'Put Yer Money Where Your Mouth Is', 'Roll It Over'
Mark Coyle: electric sitar on 'Put Yer Money Where Your Mouth Is', 12-string acoustic guitar on 'Little James'
Mark Feltham: harmonica on 'Gas Panic!'
Tony Donaldson: Mini Moog and Mellotron on 'Gas Panic!'
Charlotte Glasson: flute on 'Gas Panic!'
Produced by Mark 'Spike' Stent and Noel Gallagher
Recording engineer: Paul Stacey
Assistant engineer: Wayne Wilkins
Assistant engineer: Paul 'P-Dub' Walton
Assistant engineer: Aaron Pratley
Pro Tools operator: Jan 'Stan' Kybert
Studio assistant: Steve 'Rambo' Robinson
Recorded at Chateau de la Colle Noire, France, Olympic Studios, London, England, Supernova Heights, London, England and Wheeler End Studios, Buckinghamshire, England
UK release date: 28 February 2000
Chart placings: UK: 1, US: 24

On top of everything else going on in his life in the aftermath of *Be Here Now*, Noel quit using drugs in 1998, which would ultimately be for the best. Eventually, the songs started flowing, but Noel made a few key changes to his process.

During a 2011 interview with Chuck Klosterman, Noel admitted this album never should have been made. But that's short-changing it. While far from perfect, and their weakest album, at least up to this point, there are terrific moments on it. But it lacked motivation. Specifically, Noel lacked motivation. He was longer out to prove that Oasis were going to be the biggest and best band in the world. Noel gave an interview to Paul Lester in 2000 in which he said that songs did, in fact, start pouring out of him, but in hindsight, he has said those songs felt forced:

...But I went ahead and did it, even though I had no inspiration and couldn't find inspiration anywhere. I just wrote songs for the sake of making an album. We needed a reason to go on tour... But after that, Gem and Andy joined the band, and we started to split songwriting duties because they wanted to write songs, too. I'd slowed down as a writer and didn't feel I could keep writing 20 songs every two years.

The line at the end would foreshadow the next three Oasis albums especially, as on *Standing On The Shoulder Of Giants,* there is the only song that Noel does not write, the oft-maligned 'Little James', which was Liam's first foray into songwriting. 'Little James' aside, this album belongs to Noel. He played most of the parts on the album and played an integral role in the production of the album. The title of the album itself is a reference, perhaps, to past achievements: standing on the shoulders of giants, the giants being the previous three albums, always to be measured by what came before. In an effort to break out of the old routine, Noel purchased all new guitars and amps, and really was deliberate with the recording of this album, even if the songs were not always coming as quickly. Noel would tell *Guitar One* magazine that it wasn't the guitars that changed the sound of the album, but the amps.

For many Oasis fans, *Standing On The Shoulder Of Giants* marks the beginning of the second half of the Oasis story. If we trace the history of the band from the point at which Noel joined until the time Noel quits, this album falls approximately at the halfway point. The songs are a little different, not as consistently good perhaps, new members have joined and also left, new styles are being explored and Noel begins to slowly relinquish some control, which especially becomes evident on the subsequent records. This also marked a time in which a new Oasis album wasn't automatically a huge deal in England. The album went to number one, as did the first single, 'Go Let It Out', but there was no denying that tastes were changing. Further cementing this album as the launch of Oasis Mark II, Guigsy and Bonehead left the band before the album was recorded and Creation Records folded. Another big change was that Owen Morris was out and Mark 'Spike' Stent was in.

'Fuckin' In The Bushes' (N. Gallagher)
For an album that is known for slowing the tempo down a bit, this song certainly goes in the other direction. This is forever destined to be known not only as the opener on *Standing On The Shoulder Of Giants* but also as the opener at most subsequent Oasis concerts. Noel would cite this track and the following, 'Go Let It Out', as the two redeeming features on the album. Most fans would toss a few others in there, yet this was the first album where the songs were spotty. Even if *Be Here Now* had songs that went on a little too long and the whole thing felt a little bloated, the songwriting was still top-

notch. Because of this change in sound and, arguably, in quality, *Standing On The Shoulder Of Giants* is seen as something of a new chapter in the history of Oasis. On top of all that, 'Fuckin' In The Bushes' storms out of the gate, sounding unlike anything else in the Oasis songbook: Led Zeppelin mixed with DJ Shadow.

As one of the most danceable Oasis songs, sounding at times like a Stone Roses track, this is also one of the more acclaimed songs on *Standing On The Shoulder Of Giants*. People weren't expecting a song like this to open a new Oasis album. As Noel would say to Neil Mason for a *Melody Maker* interview in January 2000:

It started off as a B-side. The reason why that's the first track on the album is because we were thinking, 'what would be the thing you would expect most from this band?' You would expect the first single to be first. So we thought, 'Well, fuck that, let's put the first single second... It's such a non-Oasis track, but the vibe is totally Oasis.

It begins with a heavy drum beat before segueing into a sample from the Isle of Wight Festival, in which an organiser was chastising members of the crowd. The first half of the song sits in a nicely agreeable pocket before Zeppelin-esque lead guitar fills arrive about halfway through. The samples pick back up and remain for the duration of the song. It's a damn enjoyable instrumental and proves to be a highlight of the album.

'Go Let It Out' (N. Gallagher)

A-side single. Released: 7 February 2000. UK: 1

Released exactly three weeks before the album, this is the sound of a familiar Oasis but now replete with drum loops and light DJ scratching, which is actually just Noel running his fingers up and down the strings. Alan White handles the drums and Liam does the singing, with Noel doing everything else.

This is 'The first time we got close to sounding like a modern-day Beatles... which is what we were striving for years and years', said the songwriter himself. 'It's a New York hipster song... up there with the best things we've ever done', he would go on to say. In fact, Noel was in New York when he wrote the song, with the line 'the right time is always now' being lifted directly from a billboard in Times Square. Noel added touches to many of the songs on this album while in New York, with this one being no different. On top of Noel's new influences, Liam sounds different on this track. We can still tell, obviously, this is the same person who sang brilliantly on *Definitely Maybe,* but as much as Noel is changing as a writer, Liam is also changing as a singer. Having a more mature voice now, 'Go Let It Out' marks the point at which Liam masters the persona he still lives today: a slightly older, irreverent and, at times, indifferent sage, totally comfortable in his own skin. With a minute left in the song, a whistle that is blown by Noel announces a final chorus and it's hard to listen and not be excited, even after hearing it hundreds of times. Liam repeating 'don't let it in' is a highlight of the album.

Beatles references are always a dime a dozen with Oasis, yet it's hard to deny the Beatles vibe when the strings hit and Liam sings, 'Is it any wonder why princes and kings...'. What's more, the picture adorning the 'Go Let It Out' single is perhaps a Beatles homage to the *A Hard Days Night* era and the famous scenes of the Fab Four running in a field and about town. The one-two punch that opens the album is one of the most exciting in the Oasis canon, but sadly, the momentum and excitement are not maintained. The all-too-easy fan narrative is that there are about three good songs on this album, and this was the second one in as many songs.

'Go Let It Out' went to number one in the UK, and of their last five singles, including this, four went to number one. Traditionally, the first single from each album was always terrific, and the 'Go Let It Out' single carries on this tradition and includes the masterpiece 'Let's All Make Believe'. 'Go Let It Out' would be the only number-one single from the album, yet it showed that there was still an appetite for Oasis, even if the so-called moment had passed. The terrific podcast, titled Oasis Podcast, asked if 'Go Let It Out' was the best track two in the Oasis canon. While JC said it was not, and I respect his opinion, for this author, it is the best track two in the Oasis canon.

'Who Feels Love?' (N. Gallagher)
A-side single. Released: 17 April 2000. UK: 4

While not as exciting as the preceding two songs, this is an interesting track musically and introduces sounds that Oasis had not yet committed to tape. There is a strong Eastern influence going on with the track, which immediately brings up comparisons to The Beatles, as is common, and George Harrison in particular. The easiest comparison here is also the most apt; the similarities to 'Within You, Without You' are uncanny, with the sitars, tablas and the ragga feel of the song being a homage to the 1967 Harrison-penned track. Oasis would, in fact, cover this song in 2007 for a BBC tribute of sorts to *Sgt. Pepper's Lonely Hearts Club Band*. As well as all of this, Paul Stacey's bass and backwards guitar playing are further highlights.

The song is something of a litmus test for *Standing On The Shoulder Of Giants*. For people who like the experimentation, Liam's slightly new vocal sound and the production values, 'Who Feels Love?' is a refreshing and welcome change. For others, it's emblematic of everything that was wrong with the album.

'Who Feels Love?' is Thailand meets New York City, in a literal and metaphorical sense. Upon deciding he wanted to give up drugs, Noel embarked on a trip to Thailand with his wife, an acoustic guitar and a tape recorder. Inspired by temples – he would be quick to tell people that it was not necessarily the spiritual or religious aspect – the Eastern feel and hippie-esque lyrics were inspired by Thailand:

I was sort of coming out of the biggest hangover I've ever had, a 14-year hangover, I would look up and down the beach and think, 'Yeah, I do love my wife, I do love myself and life is fucking good, man. It's not all about sex and drugs and rock and roll'. You're around all these really spiritual people and it's … there's a line in it, 'my spirit has been purified', there you go. Old hippy bastard.

The final mix of the song would be further influenced by Noel's time in New York and the fast-paced vibe of the city, which inspired him to increase the song's tempo, as he attempted to capture the hustle and bustle and energy that he was experiencing on his nightly walks.

Released as a single in April 2000 and peaking at number four on the charts, 'Who Feels Love?' is the first song on the album that arguably overstays its welcome. On the flip side, Irish musician Rob Smith has allegedly called this the most underrated song of all time. While it's likely not appearing on many 'best of' lists, it's an interesting song that sees Noel penning solid lyrics and experimenting with sounds that make *Standing On The Shoulder Of Giants* an exciting listen. Check out the Japanese edition of the single for a demo version of 'Gas Panic!'. For Liam fans, the 'Who Feels Love?' music video is very Liam-heavy and includes some nice desert shots.

'Put Yer Money Where Your Mouth Is' (N. Gallagher)
If 'Who Feels Love?' saw Noel trying to stretch out as a lyricist with relatively successful results, 'Put Yer Money Where Your Mouth Is' is simply a loud song, replete with some pronounced keyboards and words that operate more like a mantra than actual lyrics.

Noel said he was going for a '20th Century Boy' by T-Rex vibe, as well as attempting to capture a 1960s garage-punk energy, which would have worked better without the prominent keyboards. P.P. Arnold was brought in on background vocals in order to fulfil this garage-punk desire. She is also featured on 'Fuckin' In The Bushes' and 'Roll It Over'. Some have accused the song of ripping off 'Roadhouse Blues' by The Doors, but much of that comes down to Liam's emphasis on the line, 'and your hands right upon the wheel'. Noel has admitted that the lyrics don't mean much of anything and he simply never got around to finishing them. Liam's vocal delivery and the verve of the guitars and crashing cymbals give this song enough juice to stay afloat.

'Little James' (Liam Gallagher)
Perhaps the most maligned song in the Oasis canon, 'Little James' is notable for being Liam's first foray into songwriting and is an easy target for fans 'and Noel' to mock. However, 'Little James', while certainly not being a great song, is better than the narrative that surrounds it. If you go into the track expecting one of the worst Oasis songs ever, you may be pleasantly surprised. Having said that, do not expect anything remotely positive from the lyrics,

which border on the ridiculous. In his defence, it was written for his stepson, a child, and the lyrics attempt to capture some of that innocence. Notably, Liam had co-written a song with John Squire in 1997, but this was his first songwriting credit on an Oasis record.

Liam was always known as a man who never sat down. As such, it was nearly impossible for him to ever commit this song to tape, despite the fact that, as Noel claims, the chords for 'Little James' had been bouncing around inside of Liam's head for years. When describing all the songs for the album to *Melody Maker* in a 2000 interview, Noel recalled:

> He was saying that he wanted that song to be an acoustic number, which is not how I remember it at all. Eventually, I sat him down and he played it acoustically. We worked out an arrangement because he had about 50 verses for it and it went on for ages... I said, 'what do you want it to sound like?', and he just said he wanted it to sound like The Beatles. So, we went, 'we can do that'. And that's what we did.

The outro features a solid guitar solo and some obligatory 'na na na's, which would lead some people to force a 'Hey Jude' comparison, as that song was also inspired by a child. Liam would semi-perfect his straightforward songwriting techniques with 'Songbird', but this minor effort is better than what most people would have you believe. You can easily track down a version that was performed by Liam in 2000 for a Portland radio station with accompaniment by Andy Bell. The track works well as a totally stripped-down song. As Noel would say, this was a nice way to wrap up the first side of the album, which he felt was the 'light and uplifting' side.

'Gas Panic!' (N. Gallagher)

If *Standing On The Shoulder Of Giants* is an album of two sides, as many say it is, with side A being the light and uplifting side, side B could not open with a better, more haunting track than this – a true fan favourite. While it is hard to say whether or not this should have been released as a single, most fans say this is, without question, the best song on the album. Containing some of Noel's best lyrics, the opening stanza is especially powerful:

> What tongueless ghost of sin crept through my curtains?
> Sailing on a sea of sweat in a stormy night
> I think he don't know my name but I can't be certain
> And in me he starts to confide

That opening line is very similar to a stanza in 'The Sphinx' by Oscar Wilde,

> What songless tongueless ghost of sin crept
> through the curtains of the night

Wilde suggests that this 'ghost of sin' is following him, that he can't escape, visiting him every night, and Noel could certainly relate. Written by Noel in London as he was withdrawing from an array of substances, namely cocaine, it was a period of his life in which he was suffering from severe panic attacks, unable to sleep consistently and waking up in cold sweats when he could sleep. Noel considered all of this, likely correctly, to be his body going through withdrawals. Noel would say of this period, and of 'Gas Panic!' specifically:

> I was trying desperately to see if I could make it any easier on myself. There's only one way to do it, which is to lock the doors, put the kettle on, sit down and wait for the demons to come. So that was written in the midst of a panic attack one morning at about five o'clock.

Prior to 1:23, the song coasts along relatively lightly with acoustic guitar, light percussion and sound effects. The remainder of the song becomes a swirling, psychedelic masterpiece replete with guitar solos, some terrific Noel background vocals and a great Liam vocal. The outro features an array of sounds before settling back down to silence. The live version on *Familiar To Millions* is perhaps even more powerful, with Liam stealing the show. His delivery of 'panic is on the way' is simply one of his greatest moments on record. The song was dropped from setlists after 2002 but remains one of the most beloved songs in the canon, worth adding to your next playlist at all costs.

'Where Did It All Go Wrong?' (N. Gallagher)

One of the unsung heroes of the album, this track was arguably better in its stripped-down acoustic format, which fit the mood and lyrics perfectly. Nonetheless, this still winds up being an unsung highlight of the album. Noel initially wanted this to be the title of the album but thought it would put too much emphasis on the track. In hindsight, Noel was wise in his decision, simply because it prevented a thousand headlines with some variation of 'where did it all go wrong?', given the, at times, negative reaction to the album.

Intended by Noel to be a companion song with 'Sunday Morning Call', and thus intentionally positioned one in front of the other on the album, Noel sings lead on both: 'They come as a pair because they are about a certain person. I can't tell you who it is; all I can say is they're fucking really famous and successful, but really fucked up at the same time'.

The song is 100% Noel Gallagher from start to finish, save for Alan White on drums. It begins as a mid-tempo song, with layers of electric and acoustic guitars. The chorus, starting at 1:07, is archetypal Noel: loud, catchy and a little soaring. A high-pitched guitar solo enters during the second half of the track, in between Noel going through the chorus three times in the outro. Noel claims that the reason he sings the track is because Liam, lacking the dynamism in his voice, could not keep up with the shifting melody.

Released as a radio single in the United States, the song did not do much chart-wise. It was performed live in a relatively stripped-down format on the first part of the *Standing On The Shoulder Of Giants* tour, but dropped after Noel, once again, left the band temporarily, with the song never to return to an Oasis setlist. The track would fit perfectly as part of a Noel Gallagher's High Flying Birds setlist and would be a nice deep-cut to mix things up and keep the crowd guessing a bit.

'Sunday Morning Call' (N. Gallagher)
A-side single. Released: 3 July 2000. UK: 4

One of the few underwhelming Oasis singles, and, quite frankly, an odd choice for release as a single in the first place. Noel has gone as far as saying that he hates the song. While doing an interview with Radio X in 2021, he was asked why he disliked the song so much: 'Because it's shit. I hate that song'. He would elaborate on this sentiment, rewording the phrase several more times and suggesting he wants to simply forget that the song exists.

Sure enough, the track is included on the singles collection *Time Flies...1994-2009*, but it is a hidden track, following two minutes of silence at the end of the final track on disc two, 'Falling Down'. *Standing On The Shoulder Of Giants* is unique in that there were not necessarily any clear-cut made-for-radio singles, save for 'Go Let It Out'. As such, 'Who Feels Love?' followed as the second single, an impressive song in many ways, but not necessarily screaming out for radio play. When it was time for a third single, Noel chose this. Would 'Gas Panic!', 'Where Did It All Go Wrong?' or 'Roll It Over' have been better? It is futile to ponder such things. Had it not been released as a single and simply acted as an album track, it likely would have fared better in the public eye.

Acting as a companion piece to 'Where Did It All Go Wrong?', which is about a specific person, 'Sunday Morning Call' is the morning-after song. Noel slips his shoes on and begrudgingly heads out of his door to interact with this unnamed person who is wasting their life away. The placement of the track does not do it any favours either, with Noel taking lead vocals on both songs and perhaps depriving fans of Liam for one song too many. As another mid-tempo track, directly after another, it causes the album to drag more than it could afford to. The solo, starting at 3:09, gives the song a much-needed energy boost.

This, like 'Who Feels Love?', peaked at number four on the charts, the worst performance of a single, chart-wise, since 'Cigarettes & Alcohol'.

'I Can See A Liar' (N. Gallagher)
A forgotten track by all but the most ardent Oasis fans. Being guitar-heavy, it garners comparisons to AC/DC, especially in the first few seconds of the song with the start/stop guitar intro. Noel would prefer to call it Sex Pistols-esque and said he was tempted to turn the song into a Sex Pistols-type rant. Relatively

similar to 'Put Yer Money Where Yer Mouth Is' in its rocking nature, the basic melody of the verse sounds a lot like 2008's 'The Shock Of The Lightning'. The lyrics are a bit lazy, especially the chorus of, 'I can see a liar, sitting by the fire'. Nonetheless, the whole band seem to be enjoying themselves, and it's a nice change of pace after the two slower Noel-sung tracks.

It is one of the shorter songs on the album and one of the songs without an overly long outro. Randomly, the song was selected as the showcase song from the new album when they performed on *The David Letterman Show* in 2000.

'Roll It Over' (N. Gallagher)

If 'Gas Panic!' is the usual choice for best song on the album, 'Roll It Over' is the real forgotten gem.

A slow-rolling, lightly strummed intro takes us to Liam singing, 'I can give a hundred million reasons'. The lyrics are open to interpretation, especially lines such as:

Look around at all the plastic people
Who live without a care
Try to sit around my table
But never bring a chair

Is this Noel commenting on the people around him, such as on 'Where Did It All Go Wrong?' and 'Sunday Morning Call'? Around this time, Noel was beginning to examine his life and those who he had surrounded himself with. People who were sitting around his table and never bringing a chair – they took from him and gave him very little in return.

Paul Stacey, whose fingerprints are all over this album, plays perhaps the best guitar solo on any Oasis record. As Noel would recall:

...The guitar solo isn't actually played by me, it's played by a friend of mine. I was having quite a bit of fucking trouble working out a guitar solo, me not being Jimi Hendrix and Gem not being involved at the time, so I said to him, 'Can you show us something to fucking play?'. He said, 'What do you want it to sound like?'

Noel would instruct Stacey to play a David Gilmour-type solo, which Stacey does brilliantly. The backing vocals during the solo add a Floyd feel as well.

The song has a similar outro to 'Gas Panic!', with the mayhem of the song slowly fading into silence. Noel would equate it to 'the old Verve before they went all poppy'. This is Noel's favourite song on the album and a very prescient choice for an album closer, with some fans hearing similarities to the far more popular 'Champagne Supernova'. Oasis had a tradition of terrific album closers, and this song continued that trend.

While never a part of Oasis setlists, Liam has brought it into his shows recently as a major treat for fans, with an especially powerful version being played at Knebworth in 2022.

Standing On The Shoulder Of Giants B-Sides/EPs

'Let's All Make Believe' (N. Gallagher)
B-side of 'Go Let It Out'

In February 2007, *Q Magazine* ran a cover story titled '500 Greatest Lost Tracks'. The premise was simple: they were ranking the best songs that were forgotten as album tracks, or in most cases, songs that were hidden away as B-sides or tucked away on deluxe versions, or demos that only appeared on box sets, etc. The list is fascinating and can be easily accessed on Rocklist.net. Sitting atop the list at number one is the Oasis track 'Let's All Make Believe'. While the praise gets a little hyperbolic at times, this is a damn good song and is essential for any Oasis B-sides playlist.

One wonders how differently *Standing On The Shoulder Of Giants* would have been received had this song been included on the album. *Q Magazine* flat out said it would have received another full star simply for the inclusion of 'Let's All Make Believe'. Noel has been criticised many times over the years for relegating superior songs to B-sides. 'Let's All Make Believe' and 'The Masterplan' tend to be cited as the two most obvious instances of that. Leaving 'The Masterplan' off of *(What's The Story) Morning Glory?* tends to be easier to forgive, as the album was already bursting at the seams with great songs. But running with this hypothetical question dealing with 'Let's All Make Believe', what song would it replace? 'Little James' may be too easy of an answer, even though it is true that it may have worked better tucked away as a B-side. Noel likely would not have replaced any of the rocking tunes on the album, as it was already short on those. Given his subsequent hate of 'Sunday Morning Call', and the fact that it drags a little, this is perhaps the slot to place 'Let's All Make Believe'.

All of this aside, this song is incredibly powerful, containing some of Noel's greatest lyrics and some of Liam's most powerful singing. The Noel-sung demo version is almost equally powerful, however – his voice fits perfectly with the lyrics and mood of the song. On the whole, for any complaints about this era of Oasis music, Noel was writing some of the best lyrics of his career. Given the recent departure of band members, and the roller coaster of a relationship that Noel and Liam enjoyed, the lyrics are easy to read into, especially the chorus: 'let's all make believe, that we're still friends and we like each other'. At 3:53, this song does not overstay its welcome and the outro does not drag on, which can't be said about every Oasis song. It almost feels too short.

This would be the only B-side from the *Standing On The Shoulder Of Giants* era that Liam would sing on. As Oasis was moving along in the second half of their career, Noel would take lead much more on album tracks and continue to sing a lot of B-sides.

'(As Long As They've Got) Cigarettes In Hell' (N. Gallagher)
B-side of 'Go Let It Out'

This is a bit of a forgotten gem, as most of the conversation around the 'Go Let It Out' single centres around 'Let's All Make Believe'. That's a shame, as this is a great B-side that is very much a product of its time and would have been an effective addition to the LP. A major 'Strawberry Fields Forever' vibe permeates the track, largely due to the flute Mellotron. Slow and purposefully lazy-sounding, the song also features another Beatles trick with the backwards guitar loop playing throughout.

This is exactly the type of song that Noel was meant to sing and he somehow manages to sound indifferent, yet fully convinced of everything he says. The verses are simple, consisting of just three chords with the bass guitar, also played by Noel, providing an oddly effective accompaniment. The end of the tune features Noel coughing, and as the cough fades away, the Middle-Eastern roots of the song really shine through.

'One Way Road' (N. Gallagher)
B-side of 'Who Feels Love?'

Many of the B-sides, starting with the *Be Here Now* era, are long forgotten by all but the most ardent Oasis fans. *The Masterplan* collected B-sides from Oasis singles associated with their first albums, the bulk of the songs coming from 1994 and 1995. Given there was never a *The Masterplan* Part II, it was nowhere near as easy to hear the B-sides from the albums following *Be Here Now*, unless, of course, you were purchasing the singles. The second single from *Standing On The Shoulder Of Giants*, 'Who Feels Love?' is nowhere near as strong as 'Go Let It Out'.

Another Noel-sung track, this fits the mid-tempo mode of many songs from this era, although this winds up being one of the criticisms of the track. It's too similar to a lot of the other album tracks and B-sides that Noel sang and this track, while solid enough, fails to really excite anyone. However, Paul Weller chose to cover this song on his 2004 album *Studio 150*. Weller's version sounds a bit more polished and radio-ready than the Oasis B-side.

'Helter Skelter' (J. Lennon, P. McCartney)
B-side of 'Who Feels Love?'

By this point, Oasis had officially covered two Beatles songs and more could be found via bootlegs, such as 'Help!' and 'Day Tripper'. In 2007, Noel would cover 'All You Need Is Love' and 'Strawberry Fields Forever' during stripped-down, acoustic shows that usually included Gem. Noel had played with Paul McCartney as a member of the Smokin' Mojo Filters when they recorded 'Come Together' for *The Help Album*, designed to help the charity War Child. Yet, both Gallagher brothers were clearly obsessed with John Lennon. Some of the most canonical Oasis concert footage of all time features Liam bowing down to a projected picture of John Lennon

as 'Live Forever' ends. Beatles comparisons had long become rote at this
point, and while no one would question their fandom, it got old at times.
It was perhaps only a matter of time before they would arrive at this 1968
McCartney-sung rocker. It is a rather disappointing offering, not nearly as
spirited as one would expect, and while it is not always true, having Liam
take lead would have likely bolstered this performance. The song would be
performed live by Oasis at different intervals in their career, most notably
on the *Standing On The Shoulder Of Giants* tour in 2000. Noel delivers
another faithful rendition that would appear on the *Familiar To Millions*
live album, closing out disc two on the standard double disc release. The
net end result was, up to that point, the most disappointing single since the
Definitely Maybe era, if not their entire career.

'Carry Us All' (N. Gallagher)
B-side of 'Sunday Morning Call'
Another single in which Noel takes lead vocals on the two B-sides, and given
he sings 'Sunday Morning Call', this means that all three songs on this release
are sung by Noel. 'Carry Us All' is one of the stronger B-sides from the era
and it's a bit of a surprise that it's not more well-known. As has been stated
before when speaking about the *Standing On The Shoulder Of Giants* era,
the lyrics are some of Noel's most effective as he bares his feelings about
organised religion:

Everybody's gone for quick, sure fire solution
But faith in any god will only bury us all

Beginning acoustically, with individually plucked strings before landing
on a G chord, the mid-tempo verses are comparable in feel to other Noel
songs from the era. At 0:36 into the song, Noel sings the bridge, 'they got me
running in and out of time', acting as the first part of the chorus, which is
simultaneously restrained and at the top of his lungs. This would have been a
much stronger A-side than 'Sunday Morning Call', even though it shares much
of the same vibe. Another song that would be perfect for Noel to perform in
2023 and another gem that has been forgotten by most fans.

'Full On' (N. Gallagher)
B-side of 'Sunday Morning Call'
Where the B-sides on the 'Who Feels Love?' single are relatively weak, the
B-sides on 'Sunday Morning Call' are anything but weak. 'Full On' is a great
Noel rocker, starting at a slow build like other great rocking numbers such
as 'Morning Glory' and 'Acquiesce'. A keyboard enters, not unlike in 'Put
Yer Money Where Yer Mouth Is', and we're off with crunching guitars. In
the *Standing On The Shoulder Of Giants* era, it has become too easy to say
two things: that Liam should have sung certain songs and that certain songs

should have made it onto the album. In this case, both points are valid. While Noel does a great job here, a rocker like this was built for Liam to sing and it's a shame we don't have a version of him doing this. 'Full On' could have worked on the album, but it would have likely relegated 'Put Yer Money Where Yer Mouth Is' to a B-side, as the songs have a similar energy and would have played the same role on the album. Most fans would agree that the two B-sides included here are better than 'Sunday Morning Call'.

Familiar To Millions (2000)

Personnel:
Liam Gallagher: lead vocals
Noel Gallagher: guitar, vocals
Gem Archer: guitars
Andy Bell: bass
Alan White: drums
Zeb Jameson: keyboards
UK release date: 13 November 2000
Chart placings: UK: 5, US: 182

The first official live album from Oasis, taken from a show at Wembley Stadium on 22 July 2000, with the version of 'Helter Skelter' being culled from Milwaukee, Wisconsin. This 90-minute double disc release gives a pretty accurate portrait of what an Oasis concert during the *Standing On The Shoulder Of Giants* tour would look and sound like, at least in terms of a setlist. Four songs are played from the new album and one song from *Be Here Now*, with everything being a cover or from the first two albums 'including single releases'. Unfortunately, most streaming services only have 'The Highlights Version' of the album, which whittles the track list down to 13 songs and cuts out 'Hey Hey, My My (Into The Black)' – the only song found here that is not found anywhere else.

The concert is perhaps most famous for Liam's extensive bantering throughout the evening, almost to the point where it was comical. Comments about Bob Geldof, calling Wembley a shithole and Noel leading a chant of 'who the fuck is Andy Bell?' are but just a few of the many highlights. Full transcripts are readily available and are worth checking out.

Perhaps most notably, at least for collectors, the album was released simultaneously on six different formats, including the now coveted and collectable double Minidisc.

'Hey Hey, My My (Into The Black)' (Neil Young, Jeff Blackburn)
Noel has never hidden his love for Neil Young and both employ a similar philosophy to guitar playing: it's not how you play, it's what you play, with neither being the flashiest of guitar players. Neil Young And Crazy Horse influences can be found on several canonical Oasis songs. This track, originally released on Neil Young's 1979 masterpiece *Rust Never Sleeps*, is a perfect fit for Oasis. While the band lacks some of the garage-rock charms that Crazy Horse possesses, this is still a terrific rendition, with Noel handling lead vocals.

Originally, Oasis were covering this song as a tribute to Kurt Cobain during the American stops on the tour. It worked so well, however, that Noel decided to keep it in the setlist when they came back to Europe. The most famous lyrics in this song, 'It's better to burn out than fade away', were famously quoted by Kurt Cobain in his suicide note. Neil Young was so shaken by this that he dedicated his underrated album *Sleeps With Angels* to Cobain.

Noel has had a strange relationship with Nirvana and Kurt Cobain. Earlier in his career, he cited Cobain and, specifically, the song 'I Hate Myself And I Want to Die', as direct inspirations for 'Live Forever' and the general Oasis mentality. This influence, however, was negative in that Noel was inspired to be *unlike* Cobain, as Noel embraced fame and popularity, in stark contrast to the grunge legend. Yet, in recent years, he has changed his tune and Noel has had nothing but positive things to say about Cobain, explaining to *NME* in 2017: 'I always had an affinity with him because he was left-handed, he had blue eyes, he was a Gemini and he was into The Beatles, and that's what I was so I was like, fucking hell'.

Mark Coyle, the co-producer of *Definitely Maybe*, did monitors for Teenage Fanclub when they went on a world tour with Nirvana. Gallagher would recall asking Coyle about Cobain, with Coyle responding that he was great and that Cobain and Noel would have gotten along splendidly. If only this meeting had occurred.

Heathen Chemistry (2002)

Personnel:
Liam Gallagher: lead vocals
Noel Gallagher: guitar, vocals
Gem Archer: guitars
Andy Bell: bass
Alan White: drums
Guest musicians:
Paul Stacey: Mellotron on 'The Hindu Times', piano on 'Force Of Nature', 'Hung In A Bad Place' and 'Better Man', Hammond organ on 'Little By Little'
Mike Rowe: piano on 'Stop Crying Your Heart Out' and 'Born On A Different Cloud', pump organ on 'She Is Love', Hammond organ on '(Probably) All In The Mind', 'She Is Love' and 'Born On A Different Cloud'
Johnny Marr: guitar solo on '(Probably) All In The Mind', slide guitar on 'Born On A Different Cloud', guitars and backing vocals on 'Better Man'
London Session Orchestra: strings on 'Stop Crying Your Heart Out'
Produced by the band
Recorded at Wheeler End
Mixed by Mark 'Spike' Stent
Recorded by Jan 'Stan' Kybert
Pro Tools engineer: Jan 'Stan' Kybert
Assistant engineer: David Treaheam
Engineering: Paul 'P-dub' Walton
UK release date: 1 July 2002
Chart placings: UK: 1, US: 23

2001 saw Oasis as road warriors as they embarked on the *Tour Of Brotherly Love* with The Black Crowes and Spacehog and earlier in 2001, they played *Rock In Rio*, which also featured Neil Young And Crazy Horse. Setlists were relatively short and tended to focus on the hits. The Black Crowes and Oasis had little in common musically but were both fronted by brothers who had, at times, volatile relationships. By almost all accounts, the tour was a blast for the bands, with relationships between the groups being great. Oasis went on before The Black Crowes, and then Gem and Noel would come out later during The Black Crowes set to play a variety of fun and famous covers. They even spruced up the setlist a little, adding in fan favourites like 'Slide Away'. Later that year, Oasis would embark on a UK tour titled *Ten Years Of Noise And Confusion*. The setlists were excellent and they were playing 'The Hindu Times' and 'Hung In A Bad Place', which would eventually be released on *Heathen Chemistry*. Furthermore, Noel had made some disparaging comments about a new Liam song, 'Songbird', initially calling it a waste of plastic. He would later revise his comments, but the fans knew that new music was being written. 2001 would see no new Oasis music being officially released. Despite this, 2001 was a crucial year for the band. The post-*Be*

Here Now years through to 2000 were tough for the band and for Noel in particular. Now, however, he had bandmates who were helping him in terms of songwriting and the band did two enjoyable tours in 2001, which returned some fun and enjoyment into their lives. The band wanted to release a new single at the end of the year, and 'The Hindu Times' was obviously written, but new band dynamics meant that Noel wasn't the dictator he once was and it appears it was harder to get a decision made in terms of a new single. 'The Hindu Times' would be released in April 2002 and was the first new slice of Oasis music since 2000. Gem had given Noel some advice, which boiled down to: 'the new single should sound exactly like what everyone wants Oasis to sound like'.

Noel has described *Standing On The Shoulder Of Giants* and *Heathen Chemistry* as his divorce albums, albums where he had nothing left to write about as he had everything that he wanted:

I had a big house in the country, I had money. I wasn't going to write about getting divorced. Let's not confuse anger with fucking misery. Great pop music – apart from the odd masterpiece, like 'Ghost Town' or 'Love Will Tear Us Apart' – is generally uplifting.

Both of these middle albums, as Noel would refer to them, did have a handful of great songs, but they lacked the cohesion and consistency of the first three albums, especially the first two. The B-sides, even, continued to drop a bit in quality during this era and never returned to their former glory. *Standing On The Shoulder Of Giants* was the first album in which anyone besides Noel wrote a song, yet *Heathen Chemistry* is the first time where it feels like the entire band is contributing songs and ideas. Furthermore, where *Standing On The Shoulder Of Giants* has its defenders and has turned into something of a cult classic, *Heathen Chemistry* would likely win the straw poll of least favourite Oasis album. Driving this point home, Liam himself ranked it as the weakest of all Oasis albums in a 2017 interview.

Heathen Chemistry is the only Oasis album where it feels as if the band are actively trying to hit every corner of what makes Oasis famous and putting it on one album. Almost to atone for what Noel felt were the weaknesses of the previous record, they actively had at least one ballad, rocker, instrumental, Noel song, Liam song, etc. *Heathen Chemistry* was produced solely by Oasis and perhaps lacked a bit of self-aware quality control. One thing that is present on *Heathen Chemistry* that is, by and large, lacking on the previous two records is a sense of joy. Despite the merits of the last two records, there are not many uplifting, fun tracks and no real concert staples had been added to the repertoire since the *(What's The Story) Morning Glory?* B-sides. *Heathen Chemistry*, as uneven as it is, added a handful of Oasis anthems to the repertoire and made it fun to be an Oasis fan again, despite some major hiccups on their 2002 tour, especially in America. These incidents included Liam losing his voice for a total of three gigs and a car crash that would cut the tour short. The most impactful net effect of *Heathen Chemistry* is that it finds Oasis Mark II as a fully formed band, once again with a number-one album and sold-out concerts all over the world, and with no signs of slowing down. *Heathen Chemistry* is certainly not the best Oasis album, and maybe it is the worst Oasis album, but it is an important album in the band's story and it is an album that, in many ways, needed to be made.

'The Hindu Times' (N. Gallagher)
A-side single. Released: 15 April 2002. UK: 1
The first single from the previous album hit number one, as did this, the first single from *Heathen Chemistry*. Oasis fan and journalist Stephen Thomas Erlewine would opine that the last three albums had their best song released as the first single, all reaching number one. Some may argue that 'The Hindu Times' is not the best song on this album, but few would argue that it is a glorious opening track. And, refreshingly, really about nothing at all, as the lyrics here matter far less than the swirling guitars. Noel allegedly got the song title from a T-shirt that he either saw in a charity shop or during a magazine cover story, depending on which version of the story you read. Released two and half months before *Heathen Chemistry* was scheduled to hit shelves, 'The Hindu Times' gave fans and critics alike hope for a strong new album. Around the same time that the single was released, the entire album was leaked online, surely impacting sales and blunting some of the excitement around future singles and the album release itself. This was certainly one of the most straightforward singles that Oasis would ever release and was a case of Noel consciously giving the people what they wanted.

The music video was apparently set to be filmed in New Delhi, matching some of the Indian undertones of the song, as well as the cover of the single. Ultimately, the music video was filmed at Abbey Road Studios and portrays a band looking as cool as ever, including a scene in which Liam drinks milk right before he starts to sing. Most notably, though, towards the end of the song, we see Noel and Liam harmonise with the same microphone. A welcome sight in what was to become a more complicated future.

Of course, it would not be a new Oasis album without the usual chatter of a song sounding too similar to something by a different artist. This time around, Noel was accused of lifting the guitar riff directly from the Stereophonics song 'Same Size Feet'. Jumping to the 0:37 mark on the song, it's hard not to hear the direct similarities.

'Force Of Nature' (N. Gallagher)
In many ways, this song sums up *Heathen Chemistry*: an average, yet forgettable song, with many commenting that Liam could have perhaps

improved it had he handled the lead vocal. Done as a demo during a soundcheck, this is essentially a solo Noel song written for the Jude Law vehicle *Love, Honour And Obey*. A relatively infectious stomp permeates the song, but it loses some of the momentum created by 'The Hindu Times'.

The most famous aspect of the song came in the aftermath of the album's release and one may wonder if Noel wrote this about his soon-to-be ex-wife Meg Matthews, with lines such as:

For smoking all my stash
But burning all my cash
I bet you knew right away
It's all over town that
The sun's going down
On the easy days of your life

Noel swears it's not about Meg and cites the fact that he wrote and recorded the tune in 1999, before the pair split, as proof of this. Either way, the vocals are some of Noel's most biting and whomever his vitriol is aimed at, he really meant it. Listen to the way he emphasises, 'for smoking all my stash' – it is hard not to be impressed by the emotion.

'Hung In A Bad Place' (Gem Archer)
Heathen Chemistry would mark the point at which Oasis became something of a democratic band, and this would only grow over the next two releases. Democratic in terms of songwriting credits on albums, mind you; this was still Noel's band and would continue to be. But this was the first Oasis album that felt like a band effort. The chemistry the band shared, as well as the shared songwriting duties, would continue until the band split.

This, Gem's first songwriting effort for Oasis, is a solid if forgettable, glam-inspired tune that fits Liam's voice perfectly. Gem, like Bonehead, was an incredibly versatile musician and proved to be hugely influential both in the studio and in live performances. His role as a songwriter would further grow on *Don't Believe The Truth*. Andy Bell, who joined around the same time as Gem and would play bass guitar, said the following about Gem's role in Oasis:

Oasis have completely evolved. Noel's old mates have left, he's been divorced and this really changes his own life around. He still has Liam, but his relationship with Liam is different – it's more tempestuous. He needs a less extreme mate and Gem's it. Gem chills Noel out. And that makes Oasis a more stable ship.

Perhaps more notable about this song, and certainly the most lucrative aspect of it for Gem, it was used in a Victoria's Secret commercial.

'Stop Crying Your Heart Out' (N. Gallagher)
A-side single. Released: 17 June 2002. UK: 2

The second single released from the album, and perhaps the best-known song from this era. For all of its charms, of which there are many, *Standing On The Shoulder Of Giants* did not contain any anthems in the classic Oasis vein. 'Go Let It Out' worked excellently as a single, but it wasn't a stadium-packing sing-along in the way that, say, 'Live Forever' was. One of the subplots to the *Heathen Chemistry* album was that Noel realised that he wasn't going to gain any new fans with his current songwriting efforts. Oasis fans are going to continue coming to shows, not because of new albums but because of all the goodwill that was built up between 1994 and 1996 and the songs therein. In this frame of mind, it also made sense for Noel to knock out a few more anthems, and kudos to Noel for being one of the few songwriters in history who has the ability to add anthems to a firmly established repertoire. Enter 'Stop Crying Your Heart Out'.

Beginning with a piano intro that wouldn't sound out of place as an unreleased Beethoven Sonata, Liam immediately shines as he sings, 'hold on'. There is, of course, a Noel-sung demo of the song, which is interesting in its bare-bones presentation, but thank goodness Noel gave vocal duties to Liam here. While most people remember the chorus, Noel does offer some perspective in the lyrics, notably, 'you'll never change what's been and gone'. From there, Liam and Noel do a call-and-response of sorts before arriving at what has become one of the most popular choruses in any Oasis song:

'Cause all of the stars are fading away
Just try not to worry, you'll see them someday
Take what you need, and be on your way
And stop crying your heart out

Liam delivers the chorus gently, his trademark accent as subdued as it has ever been. A subdued string arrangement fits in nicely and never feels too in your face. Some Beatles-esque backing harmonies are heard around 2:30 as the build-up to the extended outro begins. Towards the very end, a very lovely acoustic guitar is lightly plucked. At the time *Heathen Chemistry* was released, several journalists alleged overt similarities between this song and both 'Slide Away' and 'Don't Look Back In Anger'. In the mind of this author, those claims are overstated.

Released several weeks before *Heathen Chemistry* officially hit shelves, the song would peak at number two on the charts, which was surprising to some, as it was more friendly to the masses than the number-one hitter 'The Hindu Times'. The song was played on almost every stop of the *Heathen Chemistry* tour, but would eventually be phased out, and by the time of the *Dig Out Your Soul* tour, it had been dropped from the setlists. Leona Lewis recorded a version in 2009, which became a minor hit.

'Songbird' (Liam Gallagher)
A-side single. Released: 3 February 2003. UK: 3

This was the final single released from *Heathen Chemistry* and the first time that Liam was the songwriter on a single release. Counting the double A-side that came before, this means that five singles were released from *Heathen Chemistry*, which is more than any previous Oasis release. This incredible earworm of a song was written about Liam's then-fiancée Nicole Appleton, whom he would later marry and have a child with. At 2:07, it goes by faster than any other Oasis song and one is left wishing it was twice as long. Noel called this song 'perfect' and disparagingly refers to this as the only song Liam has and finds it crazy that Liam doesn't play it with Beady Eye or in other settings as a solo artist. 'Songbird' has been performed live, it's just not regularly performed live anymore. In the 'Lock The Box' interview that Liam and Noel did together, Liam had the following to say about the genesis of the song:

> I wrote that as a one-off. I was in France in this massive fucking mansion, doing our album. I went out one day and sat under a tree, had a bit of a biblical moment and that was it. Didn't do it to present (to) Noel, I just wrote it.

Where 'Little James' had been floating around in Liam's head and had to be coaxed out by Noel, 'Songbird' arrived in an instant, with Liam going on to say that the whole song took three minutes to write. Liam kept it simple musically, employing just three chords to write the song: G, G/F# and Em. The lyrics, while straightforward, are a massive leap forward from 'Little James' and the 'I've never felt this love from anyone, she's not anyone' is one of the more touching moments from Liam on record. Interestingly enough, a version apparently exists with Courtney Love whistling while Liam sings and plays guitar.

This would be a song that would remain in most Oasis setlists starting with the *Heathen Chemistry* tour and would always make for a nice, short shot of a tender Liam, usually sandwiched between two epic songs.

'Little By Little' (N. Gallagher)
Double A-side single with 'She Is Love'. Released: 23 September 2002. UK: 2

Written around the same time as 'Force Of Nature' during the initial sessions for *Standing On The Shoulder Of Giants*, this would be yet another anthemic sing-along that Noel would add to his repertoire. Notably, this is the only double A-side single that Oasis ever released, with 'She Is Love' as the other track and Noel taking lead vocals on both. In an interview conducted shortly after *Heathen Chemistry* was released, Noel was asked why Liam doesn't sing 'Little By Little', as it sounds like a Liam anthem. Noel gave a classic response:

> It's a shame 'cos that would have made it extra, extra special. When it came to him (recording the vocals), you could see he was going, 'I'm not going

to fucking get it'. And we were all willing him to get it. I went in and did a version and you could see he was sat at his desk going, 'Fucking bastard. He's got it'. But he doesn't want to do anything that's shit. That album ... all of it had to be worthy of us fucking carrying on making records.

The track is filled with some Zen-esque lyrics, to which Noel would credit smoking pot:

> True perfection has to be imperfect
> I know that sounds foolish but it's true
> The day has come and now you'll have to accept
> The life inside your head we give to you

Some have said that the lyrics are about Meg Matthews, while others have said that it is Noel's commentary on the Oasis fan base. Serving as a highlight of latter-era Oasis concerts, the song was a mainstay of the *Heathen Chemistry* and *Don't Believe The Truth* tours but was kept out of their final tour in support of *Dig Out Your Soul*. Easy to find on Oasis compilations, this tune proved that The Chief still had a muse he could turn to when necessary.

'A Quick Peep' (Andy Bell)

Slight would be the wrong word to use to describe this song. 'Interlude' would have perhaps been a more apt title for the song, as that is essentially what the song serves as: the literal divider of *Heathen Chemistry* as well as the symbolic divider. Part of this was due to the extreme length of the final song on the album, 'Better Man' – there is a hidden song that begins 33 minutes after the final track. *Heathen Chemistry* was a double vinyl release, and as such, 'A Quick Peep' starts at what would be side C.

A valid criticism that was made about *Heathen Chemistry* was that it felt a little top-heavy, with almost all of the singles appearing on the first half of the album. Fans and critics would make a similar comment when *Dig Out Your Soul* was released, as it did feel like Oasis would often front-load their albums, so that the more popular songs, and arguably the better songs, would appear on the first half of the album. A lot of the complaints that fans, critics and even the band themselves would have about *Heathen Chemistry* would deal with songs on the second half of the record. 'A Quick Peep' serves the purpose of announcing that we are entering that part of the album.

Andy Bell is credited as the songwriter here, his first Oasis songwriting credit, but it seems that it was a co-effort with Gem Archer. Gem would say about the song:

> This was a period when there was a lot of acoustic guitar playing before and after gigs. We had a big, long journey over the Alps and me and Andy just played guitar for about five hours.

The song does have a rollicking element to it, and listening to the track, you can easily picture a tour van scaling the Alps. By the time the song really gets going, it has already come to an end. The only equivalent in the Oasis catalogue is the intermetal interludes on *(What's The Story) Morning Glory?*. The musical themes presented within 'A Quick Peep' are interesting enough and more than hold up for the duration of the song, which is one of the shortest in the Oasis canon. Bell would continue to contribute as a songwriter with two tracks on *Don't Believe The Truth* and one track on *Dig Out Your Soul*, as well as a B-side on the 'Stop Crying Your Heart Out' single.

'(Probably) All In The Mind' (N. Gallagher)
A Noel-penned song, a Liam vocal, a Johnny Marr guitar part, a 1966 Beatles vibe mixed with a Stone Roses vibe – what could possibly go wrong? It's hard to pinpoint it, but the song just never really takes off. A psychedelic mood announces the start of the song, and immediately, we're hit with a bass line that sounds very similar to 'Rain', the terrific B-side by The Beatles. Liam takes lead vocals on the song, but you can hear Noel singing in harmony throughout almost the entire song to great effect. The lyrics tap back into some of Noel's philosophical musings:

Because the life I think I'm trying to find
Is probably all in the mind

Noel would ultimately be relatively dismissive of the lyrics, however, saying he wrote a vague psychedelic lyric about 'hearing people smile and all that'. Johnny Marr of The Smiths plays a very tasteful guitar solo that fits the mood of the song perfectly. Both Gallagher brothers were big fans of The Smiths, and Johnny Marr famously gifted Noel the guitar that he would compose 'Slide Away' on. Noel has grown especially close to Marr over the years and Marr has continued to feature on Noel's releases.

'She Is Love' (N. Gallagher)
Double A-side single with 'Little By Little'. Released: 23 September 2002. UK: 2
The second half of the only double A-side single that the band would ever release, 'She Is Love' is a song that is incredibly pleasant and slight but divides fans and is generally not a beloved track. The song is simple, like 'Songbird', but it does not work as effectively. On 'Songbird', Liam keeps things simple and the accompaniment is minimal. Here, even though it's a simple campfire sing-along type song, there is more going on than there needs to be. According to Noel, when Johnny Marr heard the song, he told him that it sounded like it took five minutes to write. This is either a compliment regarding his ability to write a minor hit or a critique of what was passing as an Oasis song nowadays. Noel was newly in love when he wrote and recorded the song and that comes through in the lyrics and the vibe of the song:

I was living in a hotel room and I had a new girlfriend and... you know. It's about being really, really happy on a Sunday morning. I'm chuffed with the lyrics. It's the only one I insisted on singing on.

Noel goes on to say that it's the one song on the album in which he disregards public opinion. It simply means a lot to him. The new girlfriend in question was Sara MacDonald, whom Noel would marry and have two kids with. In early 2023, the couple announced that they were divorcing. Sara engaged in several heated social media exchanges with Liam, who cited Sara as a factor in the breakup of Oasis. Noel insisted that he would never reconcile with Liam because of the things he said about his wife at the time. That was all a long way in the future when this was written on a very happy and content Sunday morning.

'Born On A Different Cloud' (L. Gallagher)
One of the album's better moments, this is an Oasis song that is truly underrated, unknown by most as it is tucked away on the lesser-known side of what is arguably their least popular album. This is certainly the most involved song that Liam wrote while in Oasis. It feels like several songs shaped into one and is referred to as a manic odyssey by Liam. It's an atmospheric song in a way that Liam had not yet demonstrated he was capable of writing. A few naysayers have accused the song of being plodding and a tad too long, but it never feels that it goes on longer than it should, like, say, many of the songs on *Be Here Now* did.

The many John Lennon references make for an entertaining listen, with some fans spending far too much time looking for similarities and hints. The lyrics deal with another one of Liam's children, with most pointing to Liam's son Lennon as the likely titular person who was born on a different cloud.

> Born on a different cloud
> From the ones that have burst round town
> It's no surprise to me
> That you're classless, clever and free

People usually cite 'classless, clever and free' as a Lennon lift. The line about living on borrowed time is a clear Lennon reference. Using the word 'hero' makes some think of 'Working Class Hero' and the line 'you're my sun and you're gonna shine' brings more Lennon comparisons. On top of all that, some commentators found the sound and different parts of the song to be reminiscent of 'Happiness Is A Warm Gun'.

As discussed elsewhere here, comparisons between Oasis and The Beatles were a dime a dozen, sometimes valid and sometimes forced. Liam was admittedly obsessed with John Lennon and his 2008 single 'I'm Outta Time' would also have a major John Lennon influence. One of the hidden gems on

Heathen Chemistry, the song was played on the *Heathen Chemistry* tour but dropped on subsequent tours.

'Better Man' (L. Gallagher)
As the chief of the band, Noel certainly has the final say in how the album is sequenced and his choice to have two Liam songs end the album feels a bit purposeful, even though he says he was impressed with 'Born On A Different Cloud'. The third Liam-penned song on the album, 'Better Man' is a straightforward rocker, easier to play and easier to write than 'Born On A Different Cloud'. Presumably, this song was written about Nicole Appleton and Liam's desire to be a better man as he embarked on his new relationship:

> I want to love you
> I want to be a better man
> I don't want to hurt you
> I just want to see what's in your hands

Liam brought a very simple song with two chords into the studio and intended to record the song in a more acoustic style. Johnny Marr was in the studio and played guitar with Gem, with Marr also providing backing vocals. Noel, not wanting to be a third guitar player on a track, contributed drums to the track. This is the least exciting of the Liam-penned songs on *Heathen Chemistry* and is perhaps the weakest song to end any Oasis record. The band are spot on and Liam sounds solid as ever, but there's not a great lyric or melody here and the whole thing winds up being forgettable at best.

'The Cage' (N. Gallagher)
Hidden track, which begins at the 33:13 mark on 'Better Man'
For those fans listening on CD, after 30 minutes of silence following 'Better Man', 'The Cage' begins at the 33:13 mark. This mid-tempo, slightly brooding song does not do much to redeem the relative let-down that 'Better Man' is. Some interesting guitar work is heard and the band, in general, are in fine form. However, this instrumental could have easily been relegated to a B-side or used as another interlude on the album. On the Japanese version of *Heathen Chemistry*, the song was given the distinction of being track 12 and 4:50 long.

Heathen Chemistry B-Sides/EPs
'Just Getting Older' (N. Gallagher)
B-side single of 'The Hindu Times'
Written and recorded during the sessions for *Standing On The Shoulder Of Giants*, this sounds like it belongs there, too: similar lyrics, similar instrumentation, similar singing. It sounds a bit like 'Sunday Morning Call', Noel purposely delivering a lazy performance. The lyrics, as given away by

the title, are simply a list of concerns or observations on getting older. These themes are similarly explored on *Standing On The Shoulder Of Giants*:

I'm staying in
I can't be bothered
Making conversation with the friends
That I don't know

Noel delivers an admirable vocal performance throughout the song, especially when he sings, 'And I bet this is how life…'. Not a bad song, per se, but lost between the twin peaks of 'The Hindu Times' and 'Idler's Dream'.

'Idler's Dream' (N. Gallagher)
B-side single of 'The Hindu Times'
A beautiful and different Noel ballad, unique in that it's the only Oasis song not to feature a single guitar, with Noel's beautiful piano playing being the only instrumentation. Because of this, it winds up being perhaps the most erroneously overlooked Oasis song. People always talk about 'Let's All Make Believe' as being forgotten, but it is not really forgotten when compared to 'Idler's Dream'. It is hard to say where it would have fit on *Heathen Chemistry*, perhaps replacing 'The Cage' as the album's hidden track. Or simply dropping into the middle of the album so more people would have heard it.

Beautiful lyrics and a gorgeous melody envelop the entire song. Ostensibly, the song is about Noel meeting the girl of his dreams or meeting a girl in his dreams. An 'idler' being defined as a habitually lazy person, Noel would delve back into this fertile topic on 'The Importance Of Being Idle':

I realise just what you are
You're an idler's dream
And you're singing Shangri-La

There is a clear reference to the famous Kinks song 'Shangri-La', the implication likely being that this person is so perfect that she's even singing Noel's favourite song. Perhaps more than any other Oasis song, however, the lyrics are less important than the beautiful melody. In its own quiet way, this winds up being one of the unsung latter-era B-sides.

'Thank You For The Good Times' (A. Bell)
B-side single of 'Stop Crying Your Heart Out'
An enjoyable, if relatively by-the-numbers, tune from Andy Bell. Bell would contribute two excellent tracks to *Don't Believe The Truth*, but during the *Heathen Chemistry* era, he was still finding his footing and figuring out his role in the band. His one contribution to *Heathen Chemistry* is the

instrumental track 'A Quick Peep', which is hard to complain about at under 80 seconds long, yet is fairly forgettable. 'Thank You For The Good Times' is a straightforward song lyrically, asking:

Who'll rise?
It would be so nice to hear you say
'Thank you for the good times'
Before the good times fly away

Liam was able to turn this basic song into something approaching memorable, but stopping just short of that. It is hard to imagine where Noel would have slotted this on *Heathen Chemistry* and it winds up as another forgotten Oasis B-side.

'Shout It Out Loud' (N. Gallagher)
B-side single of 'Stop Crying Your Heart Out'
This is another Noel ballad that sounds similar, lyrically and tonally, to the mid-tempo songs that Noel was singing during the *Standing On The Shoulder Of Giants* era. Lyrically, the song deals with a lot of typical Noel themes such as being alive, dreaming away and escapism: 'I hope at last we get some peace, I hope the light shines on we as one'. A piercing guitar solo comes in around 1:48 and has a heavy Neil Young vibe to it. A straw poll of Oasis fans would likely have this and 'Thank You for The Good Times' appearing on *Heathen Chemistry* over some of the weaker songs therein. As such, the batting average on the 'Stop Crying Your Heart Out' single is one of the higher ones from the last three albums, which is, of course, relative.

'My Generation' (Pete Townshend)
B-side single of 'Little By Little' with 'She Is Love'
In all the talk over all the years about the drama between Noel and Liam, the drama between other band members, Noel's songwriting prowess, Noel walking out during tours, Liam's wardrobe choices, etc., people often forget how good of a band Oasis were. By the time of *Heathen Chemistry*, the Gallagher brothers, Gem Archer, Andy Bell and Alan White made up what was perhaps the best-sounding iteration of Oasis in terms of how they sounded and played together. This band, especially, sounded terrific when playing rock songs and the band usually gelled perfectly when covering canonical classic rock songs such as 'Street Fighting Man'. Thus, 'My Generation', an even more famous song than 'Street Fighting Man', became another perfect vehicle for the band.

While both Liam and Noel have spoken lovingly of The Who over the years, and Noel and Liam have both performed at Roger Daltrey's Teenage Cancer Trust Benefit concert, it is sometimes surprising that they're not even bigger fans. If any classic rock legend appears to be on Noel's wavelength,

Pete Townshend seems like a pretty good candidate. Great lyrics, prolific, intelligent, opinionated, etc. Alas, Noel would be quoted as saying that *Live At Leeds* was the only Who album he could sit through from start to finish. He did, however, speak glowingly of The Who's *The Ultimate Collection*, saying The Who were up there with The Beatles, for him, in terms of guitar-based music.

As the only B-side on the single, it's a perfect addendum to the two Noel Gallagher-sung tracks that precede it. The song storms out of the gate like a punk single, the band sounding tight and loud. The first thing that the listener notices is that Liam does not try and do Daltrey's trademark stutter here. Where Daltrey says 'd-down' in the first verse of the song, Liam removes the stutter completely in this verse – probably wisely. He never holds the word 'fade' when saying, 'why don't you all fade away'. He does, however, use the Daltrey-delivery on the word 'say' 41 seconds into the song, and then turns around and uses the Daltrey stutter on the word 'generation' 51 seconds into the song. For the remainder of the song, this pattern of Liam picking strategic points at which to mimic Daltrey's delivery continues.

One of the most famous parts of 'My Generation', as performed by The Who, is the bass guitar of John Entwistle. The bass guitar is just as prominent on Oasis' version; Andy Bell performs the classic bass fills of the original and shines throughout the song. Also, of special note, the band nail the background vocals. Liam Gallagher would later tour with The Who, citing 'My Generation', 'Disguises' and 'Armenia City In The Sky' as his favourite Who songs.

While Oasis are perhaps more known for covering The Beatles, their covers of canonical songs by Slade, The Rolling Stones and The Who are incredibly captivating.

'You've Got The Heart Of A Star' (N. Gallagher)
B-side single of 'Songbird'
A solid Noel B-side ballad with that now-to-be-expected mid-tempo ballad vibe. An enjoyable song, which Tom Howard of the *NME* suggested is actually about the eldest Gallagher brother. There are several lyrics contained within the song which could give that impression, although Noel has never said as much. 'But the light never hits ya' and 'Maybe we could all just get along' are two lines that jump out when trying to justify the Paul Gallagher theory. The story of Paul Gallagher is told in the uneven but interesting book *Brothers: From Childhood To Oasis*. Paul and Liam were never close, mainly due to the age gap, but Noel and Paul enjoyed a close relationship and Noel could have certainly been signalling Paul with this song.

While few would argue that the best Oasis B-sides were associated with the singles from the first two albums, there were still gems to be found amongst the *Standing On The Shoulder Of Giants* and *Heathen Chemistry* era singles. One could make an excellent playlist simply comprised of Noel-sung Oasis B-sides exactly like this one. Noel was no stranger to acoustic ballads, but this one utilises an organ and a horn section to great effect, which differentiates 'You've Got The Heart Of A Star' from similar Noel ballads. This track has a comforting vibe to it, almost similar to 'Half The World Away'.

'Columbia (Live)' (N. Gallagher)
B-side single of 'Songbird'
A live version of the fan-favourite 'Columbia', taken from a show at the Glasgow Barrowlands from October 2001. A little less spacey than the version that appears on *Definitely Maybe,* this is a solid rendition of a song that most fans were probably excited to hear, but the new tradition of filling singles with live versions of older songs was now beginning.

'Merry Christmas Everybody' (Holder, Lea)
Non-album release as part of 1 Love/War Child compilation
The less famous of the two Slade covers, despite being the far bigger hit for Slade at the time of release. The Slade vibe and sound are a perfect fit for Oasis, which explains why 'Cum On Feel The Noize' worked so well. 'Merry Xmas Everybody', on the other hand, is likely the weakest of all of the classic rock songs that Oasis ever covered.

 NME came up with an initiative called '1 Love' in support of the War Child charity, which worked with children who had been disaffected by war. Artists were asked to select one of their favourite songs to cover; Oasis' choice of song is essentially a solo outing for Noel. Worth hearing for the completists, but better left forgotten.

Don't Believe The Truth (2005)

Personnel:
Liam Gallagher: vocals, backing vocals, tambourine, hand claps
Noel Gallagher: lead guitar, backing vocals, lead vocals (2, 5, 8), co-lead vocals (11), producer, drums (11)
Andy Bell: bass guitar, rhythm guitar, acoustic guitar
Gem Archer: rhythm guitar, lead guitar, bass guitar, keyboards, harmonica, backing vocals
Zak Starkey: drums, percussion, handclaps
Martin Duffy: piano on 'Love Like A Bomb'
Lenny Castro: percussion on 'Part Of The Queue'
Terry Kirkbride: drums and percussion on 'Mucky Fingers'
Henry Phillpotts: mixing assistant on 'Mucky Fingers'
Paul 'Strangeboy' Stacey: mixing on 'Mucky Fingers', piano and Mellotron on 'Let There Be Love'
Produced by Dave Sardy and Noel Gallagher
Recording engineer: Greg Gordon, Ryan Castle and Andy Brohard
Mastered by Ian Cooper
Recorded in London and California between December 2003 and January 2005
UK release date: 30 May 2005
Chart placings: UK: 1, US: 12

For many fans, Oasis never really went away. Their singles stayed fairly excellent and even on 'arguably' inconsistent albums, such as *Standing On The Shoulder Of Giants* or *Heathen Chemistry*, there were enough good album tracks to keep people believing. On top of that, their last three albums continued to debut at number one in the UK. For those who stopped believing, however, *Don't Believe The Truth* marks the point in the standard music-journalism narrative when Oasis returned to form. The slight irony in this return-to-form narrative is that, of the 11 tracks on the album, only five were written by Noel, which would be the fewest he would ever compose for an album. Was Noel losing his muse? Unlikely. By and large, his best songs are the strongest on the album. But even more so than *Heathen Chemistry*, which saw Noel barely writing half the songs, *Don't Believe The Truth* is perhaps the first Oasis album that feels like a full-band album. Every band member makes songwriting and arranging contributions, with Zack Starkey doing a great job keeping the beat on his only Oasis studio outing.

Of course, during promotional interviews, Noel would make familiar comments about this current album being the best one since *Definitely Maybe* and how certain songs were bonafide classics – when some clearly weren't. But with this album, more so than any since *(What's The Story) Morning Glory?*, Oasis delivered an album that worked from start to finish.

Most of the songs are good, with a handful being very good and at least two 'bonafide classics' that stand beside the much-loved earlier hits: 'Lyla' and

'The Importance Of Being Idle'. The accolades associated with *Don't Believe The Truth* are extensive and, at times, sound a little over-the-top, despite its merits. *Q Magazine* ranked it as the 4th best album of 2005, and in 2008, that same magazine would rank it as the 14th best British album of all time, as well as album 41 on their list of Top 100 Albums of the 21st Century. *MOJO* ranked it as the 25th best Recording of the Year for 2005. For much of 2005, Oasis were as popular as they had ever been, putting to bed the oft-told story that they never regained their 1994-1996 popularity. The most apt quote regarding *Don't Believe The Truth* may have come from Nick Southall, who wrote a review of the album in 2005:

> Where *Be Here Now* was a cocaine-fuelled caricature, *Standing On The Shoulder Of Giants* an attempt by Noel to develop the band despite its disintegration, and *Heathen Chemistry* a too-reactionary kick back towards the past, *Don't Believe The Truth* is simply Oasis being Oasis with maximum efficiency. Which is to say that if you're a committed acolyte of the church of Oasis, you'll love it. And if you're not, you won't give a fuck.

'Turn Up The Sun' (A. Bell)

The first track on any album is always important, but for Oasis, they were always *very* important. From 'Rock 'n' Roll Star' to 'The Hindu Times', they serve as the first impression, not counting any singles that had been released, which, of course, could also be the first track on an album. Noel must have been feeling generous, as this marks the first instance of a Noel song not opening an Oasis album. In fact, apart from the instrumental 'Fuckin' In The Bushes', the last three Oasis albums all open with the first single released from the album. With *Dig Out Your Soul,* Noel would be back to occupy the opening track. Anyone who was worried about Andy Bell's songwriting chops quickly had their fears assuaged, as 'Turn Up The Sun' winds up being one of many highlights from the album.

The opening sounds like a psychedelic bazaar of sorts, almost like a song from *The Godfather*. At 0:38 seconds into the song, the band join in; the rhythm section becomes more pronounced and the music builds up to Liam's delivery, one of the great couplets to any latter-era Oasis song:

> I carry a madness
> Everywhere I go

Andy was clearly writing for Liam; the chorus, 'love one another', is a bit cheesy, perhaps, but it fits the mood of the song and relates to many of the 1960s throwbacks found throughout the album. With the song up and running, the string section adds an extra body and warmth to the proceedings. At 2:45, the song returns to the sound of the intro as it fades out.

This was a huge leap forward from Bell's only contribution to *Heathen Chemistry*, the instrumental track 'A Quick Peep', and 'Thank You For The Good Times' from the 'Stop Crying Your Heart Out' single. It is likely the best song that Bell ever wrote while in Oasis and a terrific way to kick off the album. The song was an obvious choice as a new addition to the setlist on the *Don't Believe The Truth* Tour, often acting as the opening number directly after snippets of 'Fuckin' In The Bushes'.

'Mucky Fingers' (N. Gallagher)

Over the years, Noel has copped sounds and riffs from many recognised bands. Just on this album, there are songs directly influenced by The Kinks, The La's and The Rolling Stones. This time around, it was The Velvet Underground and their song 'I'm Waiting For The Man' in particular. On The Velvet's original version, drummer Moe Tucker is perhaps the most important person, driving the pounding rhythm forward and providing ground for Lou Reed's guitar strokes. Here, the drums are played by Terry Kirkbride, who definitely has more of a Maureen Tucker vibe than Zak Starkey, his workmanlike chops working perfectly throughout.

Gem plays a harmonica solo at 2:12 that gets a little ear-splitting towards the end, but still provides a nice contrast to the first half's musical onslaught. Noel would say of the song: 'This was the result of too many nights in the dressing room, brainwashing Gem with The Velvet Underground and then thinking, 'Fuck it! Dylan rules!''

'Lyla' (N. Gallagher)

A-side single. Released: 16 May 2005. UK: 1

In March 2005, it was confirmed that the next Oasis single, 'Lyla', would be released – the first Oasis single since 'Songbird' in 2003. In interviews around this time, Noel would describe the song, at various times, as sounding like The Who, the poppiest thing since 'Roll With It' and, perhaps best of all, 'specifically designed for pogoing'.

As the first single to be released from the album, this was, for many, a welcome return to 'Noel Gallagher the songwriter'. It is said that Noel was not initially crazy about this song, which had been floating around his head since the sessions for 'The Hindu Times', and it was only after they began playing it live that he grew to love it. Liam agreed, saying: 'I never realised how good it was until we went out and played it live'. Noel remarked: 'If you don't like that kind of thing, get the fuck out'. Noel goes on to recall that he might have started writing 'Lyla' after listening to the song 'Armenia, City In The Sky' by The Who, a great album track from *The Who Sell Out*. Noel would say while being interviewed by James Brown:

I'd written the song and it was originally called 'Smiler', but Gem already had a song called 'Smiler', so I had to change it and the only girl's name I could fucking come up with that rhymed with 'Smiler' was 'Lyla'… I had a really low period, I'd lost all enthusiasm for writing after *Be Here Now*, then *Standing On The Shoulder Of Giants* and parts of *Heathen Chemistry*. I didn't know where I was going with it. I didn't know what I was trying to fucking do, and 'Lyla' re-energised the band.

Released two weeks before *Don't Believe The Truth* would hit shelves, 'Lyla' was a smash, both critically and commercially. Reaching number one in its first week of release, it became the band's seventh number one in the UK. As a sign of renewed life in the US, it was the first Oasis song to appear on any US singles chart since 2000 with 'Go Let It Out'. 'Lyla' sees the band at a latter-day peak; Noel writing a straightforward but brilliant tune; Liam sounding as engaging as ever; Zak Starkey turning in a monster drum performance and Andy Bell and Gem Archer performing more effectively than their previous efforts. Noel provides absolutely stellar harmonies throughout the song.

A guitar solo divides the song in half, and at about 4:10, the song transitions into a fade-out, with piano and drums becoming the most prevalent sounds. Set in the key of B major, some would accuse the song of being too similar to 'Street Fighting Man' by The Rolling Stones, a song which Oasis had already released as a B-side. Alas, a majority of journalists pointing this out likely were not familiar with this B-side.

Wisely being added as a live staple immediately upon release, it would remain in the setlists throughout the remaining tours the band would do. Where it says, 'I've waited for a thousand years, for you to come and blow me off my mind', Liam would sometimes change the lyrics to 'for you to come and fuck me out my mind'. Crude but effective. Liam would add the song to his solo repertoire in 2019, which was another wise choice, as it's ostensibly an easy song to play and crowds eat it up. Included on both *Stop the Clocks* and *Time Flies…1994-2009*, for many, this and 'The Importance Of Being Idle' were the last great Oasis songs.

'Love Like A Bomb' (L. Gallagher, G. Archer)
Track four sees the first Liam songwriting contribution on the album, this one a co-write with Gem. Although acoustic, this is not as sweet or simple as, say, 'Songbird'. It's hard to believe that Liam did not have Appleton in mind when he wrote these lyrics, opening with the couplet:

I'm seeing
A whole 'nother world in my mind
Girl I'm feeling'
And breathing in love all the time

Liam tries to hit a falsetto with mixed results before a keyboard enters and gives the song a little colour. It's a pleasant enough tune and Liam does a great job of singing it, but being sandwiched between what were likely the two best songs on the album was perhaps not the greatest sequencing choice that could have been made.

'The Importance Of Being Idle' (N. Gallagher)
A-side single. Released: 22 August 2005. UK: 1

The second single released from *Don't Believe The Truth*, and at the time of this writing, the last Oasis single to hit number one. It was an impressive feat for this to hit number one right after 'Lyla' did, showing that the public still had an appetite for Oasis and were excited about the new singles. Interestingly, 2005 would be the only year that Oasis would ever have two number-one singles. Additionally, this was the only time that Oasis would have two back-to-back number one's from the same album, surprising though that may be for many. As the story goes, Noel was cleaning out a garage and stumbled upon the book *The Importance Of Being Idle: A Little Book Of Lazy Inspiration* by Stephen Robbins. Noel would specifically cite The Kinks and the song 'Clean Prophet' by The La's as the musical inspiration for the song. The lyrics were inspired by Noel dragging his feet, ostensibly being lazy, around this time in his life. The line about begging his doctor for one more line has led many to draw a connection to the story of how Noel finally gave up cocaine.

'Everything about it is fuckin' amazing', said the humble songwriter himself, Noel Gallagher. It was written about a period in the band's life in which there was uncertainty about the release date for what would become *Don't Believe The Truth*. Liam allegedly phoned Noel one day to ask about the next steps for recording songs for the album and a release date. Noel downplayed his concerns and told him to trust the process. This importance of trusting that everything will be okay, and of being a lazy bastard, gave the song its title. An interesting video was made for the song, featuring Welsh actor Rhys Ifans, but not featuring the band in any capacity. The video, populated by a slew of dancing undertakers lip-syncing to the track, is perhaps their single best music video. The song, like 'Lyla', would become a staple of almost every single subsequent Oasis concert and is still a mainstay of Noel Gallagher setlists.

A great British pop song indeed.

'The Meaning Of Soul' (L. Gallagher)
Another garage rocker, this one is driven by layers of acoustic guitars. It has an interesting chord progression, which is likely explained by the fact that Liam wrote it – his ability to write for guitar was workmanlike on a good day. The lyrics are pure Liam:

I'm different bleach and an Armani elite
I'm ten outta ten all night

As a statement of intent, declaring Liam's confidence, swagger and coolness, the song works fine. This is, in large part, due to the short length, and as such, it does not really have time to overstay its welcome. The chorus sees an interesting melody, with Starkey's drumming again being a highlight.

Often played in the first encore slot on the *Don't Believe The Truth* tour, the song would provide a nice little jolt of Liam rock 'n' roll before often leading into 'Guess God Thinks I'm Abel' and then, usually, into 'Don't Look Back In Anger'.

'Guess God Thinks I'm Abel' (L. Gallagher)

Opening with just an acoustic guitar, 'Guess God Thinks I'm Abel' quickly announces itself as another very pleasant Liam semi-ballad. Despite being, for some, one of the best rock singers of his generation, it is interesting that the majority of Liam-penned songs are slower songs, more concerned with melody and lyrics than loud guitars.

Abel, of course, is from the Old Testament, the second son of Adam and Eve and is famous for being killed by his older brother, Cain. Obviously, then, the title alone suggests that Liam and Noel's relationship is the focus here. This is exactly what people thought and still think, although the lyrics are relatively vague for those searching for direct evidence of Liam talking about Noel.

> I could be your lover, you could be all mine
> We'd go on for ever, 'til the end of time
> You could be my best friend, stay up all night long
> You could be my railroad, we'd go on and on

The relationship between Noel and Liam had always been at the heart of Oasis and this would continue through to the final show on the *Dig Out Your Soul* tour. As such, there was always a romanticism assigned to any song in which they sang together or any song that could have been about the other.

At about 2:48, the song goes near-silent for a few seconds before bursting into the final stanza of 'come on, oh, let's make it tonight'.

Was Liam suggesting that, despite his efforts, Noel continues to ignore Liam or refuses to respect him, thereby figuratively killing him? Or is this reading too far into the lyrics and this was simply Liam having a little fun with the title? The truth is likely somewhere in the middle. Noel, of course, had some wickedly disparaging remarks about the whole thing:

> Liam's gotten all religious. It's quite disturbing. He thinks he's Abel for some weird reason. He wrote a new song called 'Guess God Thinks I'm Abel'. And I thought, 'Right, so you think you're Abel. That must make me Cain. Doesn't Cain kill Abel?'

'Part Of The Queue' (N. Gallagher)
By the time *Standing On The Shoulder Of Giants* was released, Noel was singing almost as much as Liam was, especially when B-sides are considered. Of the five songs that Noel contributed to *Don't Believe The Truth*, he sings lead on three of them and co-lead on one more. Of his songs on the album, this is the one Noel composition that flies below the radar a little. Still guitar-heavy, but this time, with layered acoustic guitars, the song takes a bare-bones approach, with verses, at times, sounding not unlike 'Cruel Summer' by Bananarama or perhaps an overall vibe not unlike 'Golden Brown' by The Stranglers.

The first three Noel-written songs on the album are heavy guitar numbers that also act as throwbacks to the 1960s, with their musical references to other canonical songs from Noel's favourite decade. This winds up being the first Noel song that feels slightly run-of-the-mill, but since the batting average increased so much on *Don't Believe The Truth*, the net result is still a solid song. The lyrics seem to be about Noel's disillusionment with big city life and, a common thoroughfare in much of his work, feeling out of place:

Suddenly I found
That I'd lost my way in this city
The streets and the thousands of colours
All bleed into one

As a song that gets a little lost on side two of *Don't Believe The Truth*, one would imagine that this is the type of song Noel was referring to when he said on the interview circuit for this album:

Someone said to me my songs sound like B-sides from 1994. I take that as a compliment because the B-sides I wrote then should have been on *Be Here Now*. That would be an insult to some people, but not me.

'Keep The Dream Alive' (A. Bell)
Andy Bell was on a roll around this time, as his two contributions to *Don't Believe The Truth* are two of the unsung highlights of the album. A wistful tune with maybe just a bit of a shoegaze undertone, 'Keep The Dream Alive' is one of the best Oasis songs that no one talks about.

Prior to joining Oasis, Andy Bell was a member of the band Ride, who were one of the most influential shoegaze bands. Shoegaze itself has turned into a bit of a catch-all term to describe guitar distortion, effects and a general My Bloody Valentine-type sound. While Oasis would never be confused with having any overt shoegaze influences, Bell obviously brought such a sensibility with him when he joined Oasis and it's felt here.

The chorus of the song, first heard at 1:31, sounds like it could have fit on an early War On Drugs album with its crescending vocals. The song continues to rise for five minutes, always feeling like it is building and heading towards something, eventually settling down with a simple fade with the melody of the song replaying. The guitar solo acts as the climax of the song before Liam adds some obligatory 'na na na's.

'A Bell Will Ring' (G. Archer)

Track ten gives us the only Gem Archer songwriting credit on the album, not counting his co-write with Liam on 'Love Like A Bomb'. It also gives us one of the most overtly Beatles-esque songs on the album, along with 'Let There Be Love', which would follow and end the album. A lot of fans and journalists point out how similar the guitar work is to *Revolver*-era Beatles; once you hear the vintage crunch of the guitars, it certainly brings to mind that 1966 Beatles sound that everyone in the band clearly loved. It is an optimistic tune and the type of song that Liam could sing all day, echoing themes that had shown up in Noel's lyrics before, such as the coming of a new day and the idea that things will improve:

The sun will shine on your again
A bell will ring inside your head
And all will be brand new

Typically played every night during the *Don't Believe The Truth* tour, often right after 'The Importance Of Being Idle', this was a solid tune that has been all but forgotten by all but the most ardent supporters.

'Let There Be Love' (N. Gallagher)

A-side single. Released: 28 November 2005. UK: 2

A common critique of Oasis albums, starting with *Be Here Now*, is that they drag on towards the end, being far longer than they need to be. Most fans could easily identify two or three songs that they wouldn't mind trimming from *Standing On The Shoulder Of Giants* and *Heathen Chemistry*. *Don't Believe The Truth*, on the other hand, feels like it ends too soon. At 42:43, it is the shortest Oasis album, and due to the democratic nature of the album, it never feels like we get too much of any one type of song. The singles and radio songs on *Don't Believe The Truth* were front-loaded on the album, as per usual, but the quality is consistent nonetheless. Even so, it was obvious that a Noel song would close the album, especially with him giving the opening track away. Enter a song that had been written during the sessions for *Standing On The Shoulder Of Giants* that was initially called 'It's A Crime'. It would be the final single released from the album, and unfortunately, would not go to number one as the two previous singles had.

The most notable part of the song is the fact that Liam and Noel share lead vocals, Liam taking all the verses and Noel taking a bridge in the middle, starting with 'C'mon baby blue'. The song does drag a bit, with Noel's vocals wrapping up before the song is even halfway over, just after he holds one of the highest notes of his career with 'gonna pass you by'. A pronounced string section enters and transitions us back to an overly subdued Liam repeating the first verse and almost a dozen instances of 'let there be love'.

'Let There Be Love' is a song that divides a lot of fans; is it a late-career masterpiece or a throwaway that is mildly saved by Liam's vocals? It is certainly the weakest of the three singles released from the album and could have benefitted from some editing or at least another appearance by Noel to balance things out a bit. Only performed twice, but both times by Noel solo, the song essentially reverted to its demo version format. The music video is a nice little montage of footage from the summer of 2005, yet none of the clips actually include the band playing 'Let There Be Love'.

Don't Believe The Truth B-Sides/EPs
'Eyeball Tickler' (G. Archer)
B-side single of 'Lyla'
A nice little rocker from Gem Archer, one of the best songs he contributed to the band and likely the best B-side from the *Don't Believe The Truth* era. The 'Lyla' single is unique in that it contains three songs, each written by a different band member. 'Eyeball Tickler' is the first of two B-sides that Gem would contribute. It's a jovial, garage-rock track that would not have sounded out of place on an album by The Hives or any number of bands emerging out of New York in the early noughties. It's also similar in vibe and length to the Liam track 'The Meaning Of Soul', which is perhaps why it was relegated to a B-side. It's a shame because *Don't Believe The Truth* could have benefitted from this short track, becoming one of the strongest rockers on the album. The lyrics are a bit nonsensical:

Listen to the monkey
Feeding on your brain
I feel okay
No pain!

The lyrics do not really matter here. This song was purely an excuse for Liam to rock, and rock he does.

'Won't Let You Down' (L. Gallagher)
B-side single of 'Lyla'
The B-sides from *Don't Believe The Truth* and *Dig Out Your Soul* are the weakest of any Oasis era. 'Won't Let You Down' is one of the many B-sides that is better left forgotten. Liam, usually brilliant in his vocal delivery, struggles mightily here and this is perhaps his most nasal performance ever. The title of the song gives away what the lyrics deal with, and while it may be tempting to think that it was Liam assuring Noel, it was likely written for

Liam's girlfriend Nicole Appleton. It's a semi-acoustic song with handclaps and a flute Mellotron. The most interesting part of the song is when the strings come in just before the 2:00 mark and the song begins to fade out, the string arrangement making for a temporary lifting of spirits.

'Pass Me Down the Wine' (L. Gallagher)
B-side single of 'The Importance Of Being Idle'
Between his contributions to *Don't Believe The Truth* and the associated B-sides, this was Liam's most prolific period in Oasis, although *Dig Out Your Soul* would see similar numbers of songwriting contributions. He started coming into his own as a songwriter on *Heathen Chemistry*, and by the time of *Don't Believe The Truth,* he was contributing more material to the band than any member, save for his brother. Liam's contributions tended to fit into one of two camps: rockers like 'The Meaning Of Soul' or 'Better Man', and then more acoustic-based mid-tempo numbers like 'Love Like A Bomb' or 'Pass Me Down The Wine'.

At the very onset of 'Pass Me Down The Wine', it sounds like 'My Sweet Lord' for the briefest of seconds. This likely has less to do with a conscious effort and more to do with the fact both songs feature big, open strumming on layered acoustic guitars. Some of the rhyming couplets throughout leave a bit to be desired, but we are treated to a catchy chorus that would have fit in nicely with some of the other Liam contributions on the album. Some have speculated that the song is about Liam, or, on the other end of the spectrum, a nameless narrator at a wedding, and some of the lines in the song could clearly indicate that. The ending lyrics are classic Oasis, addressing all of mankind, or at least all the people at this party.

> To all my sisters yeah you're looking pretty fine
> And to all my brothers I bet you're feeling kinda high
> And to all my mothers well come now, don't be shy
> And to all the fathers who are sick and fucking tired

'The Quiet Ones' (G. Archer)
B-side single of 'The Importance Of Being Idle'
Gem Archer proved himself to be a competent songwriter during his time in Oasis. He allegedly claimed at one point that it was daunting whenever he had to submit a song to the band because of Noel's stature as a songwriter. Noel, however, has stated in many interviews that he enjoyed having help with songwriting duties on the last three records. 'The Quiet Ones', however, was not one of Gem's best efforts. At 2:01, it does not really overstay its welcome, given it's so short, and its acoustic nature makes it relatively benign and sweet, but it simply feels boring and like an unfinished track. The electric guitar that comes in after the verses adds a fleeting flash of something interesting, but this is a B-side that is best forgotten by all, save for the true completists.

'Sittin' Here In Silence (On My Own)' (N. Gallagher)
B-side single of 'Let There Be Love'
The 'Let There Be Love' single is the only one from the era in which Noel
wrote every song. Like 'The Quiet Ones' in length and half-finished vibe, but
a stronger song, 'Sittin' Here In Silence (On My Own)' may be the most John
Lennon-esque song that Noel ever wrote, sounding as if it was lifted from an
album such as *Mind Games*.

The lyrics deal with a desire to be alone, likely away from the circus that
had long ago become Noel's life:

Wait 'til everybody's gone
And only I can see
What it means to be
Sittin' here in silence on my own

While not as strong as 'Idler's Dream', both songs demonstrate that Noel was
still capable of writing beautiful songs that he was hiding as B-sides.

'Rock 'N' Roll Star (Live)' (N. Gallagher)
B-side single of 'Let There Be Love'
From 'Let There Be Love' onwards, the remaining singles that Oasis would
release contained live versions of songs and/or remixes to fill out the space.
Gone were the days of the near-20-minute single with 15 minutes of new songs.

Taken from the City of Manchester Stadium gig from 2 July 2005, this live
rendition of 'Rock 'N' Star' is a rocking version that sees Liam and the rest of
the band in top form.

'Who Put The Weight Of The World On My Shoulders?' (N. Gallagher)
Non-album release as part of the Goal! soundtrack
The 2005 sports drama film *Goal!* featured a soundtrack released on Big
Brother records. As such, the hope and expectation was that Oasis would be
providing new material. What ultimately happened was that two songs were
remixed and re-recorded, 'Cast No Shadow' and 'Morning Glory', and Noel
provided a solo song, 'Who Put The Weight Of The World On My Shoulders?'.
The songs are easy to find on YouTube these days but have never been
officially released elsewhere.

By this point, this is a run-of-the-mill Noel ballad, replete with heavy strings
that either enhance the track or detract from it, depending on your point of
view. For this author, they are enjoyable, if a bit cheesy.

'Can Y'See It Now? (I Can See It Now!!)' (N. Gallagher)
Bonus Track for Japanese Edition of *Don't Believe The Truth*
Released as a bonus track in Japan, this song is most notable for being a
signpost of things to come in Noel's solo career, with more diverse influences

than Oasis typically explored. Essentially, this is an instrumental track, save for Noel repeating the title of the song a few times. Not a bad song, if perhaps a bit repetitive, this one is for the completists only.

Stop The Clocks (2006)

Besides Noel feeling an immense sense of relief, the most consequential result of the Sony contract ending was that it paved the way for the inevitable release of a compilation. Noel had said on numerous occasions that the band would not release a greatest hits album unless they were about to split up or had split up, depending on the interview. Given things had not ended yet in 2006, and the release was inevitable, Noel got involved as curator and changed the concept from greatest hits to a best of, as he felt a collection of some singles, key album tracks and key B-sides would be better than simply a compilation of singles. This would be confirmed to fans, eventually, when *Time Flies...1994-2009* was released and failed to work as well as *Stop The Clocks*.

In the endlessly fascinating and informative interview 'Lock The Box', Noel justifies this release by saying that a 'best of' is different from a greatest hits and, therefore, acceptable. Noel selected the tracks, and according to Liam in the same interview, he 'just fuckin' done it' without consulting anybody. 'There's never an Oasis meeting, there's a Noel Gallagher meeting', according to Liam. The main procedure involved simply going through the songs that commonly appeared in Oasis setlists through to the most current tour. While any compilation culled from the catalogue of a band with many songs is sure to provoke some minor outrage, *Stop The Clocks* does a relatively fine job of serving as a pretty decent 'best of'. There were some curious choices made by Noel, however. While it was never a fan-favourite single, the exclusion of 'Roll With It' seems odd, as does 'Shakermaker'. Nothing at all from *Be Here Now*, not even an edited 'Stand By Me', 'Don't Go Away' or 'D'You Know What I Mean?'. No 'Little By Little' or 'Stop Crying Your Heart Out' from *Heathen Chemistry* and plenty of essential B-sides left off. With both discs staying under 45:00 in length, it was not an issue of space either. The issue was allegedly trying to preserve the flow of the album and including something like 'D'You Know What I Mean?' would have upset the flow. Nonetheless, these are 18 phenomenal songs and Noel knows it, with one press release referring to the collection as a dream setlist. The focus is, of course, on the first two albums, that era accounting for 14 of the 18 tracks. A song like 'Whatever' was likely kept off due to the copyright complexity. On the Japanese version, 'Roll With It' and 'Let There Be Love' were included, and on an iTunes edition, fans would hear 'Cast No Shadow' and 'Columbia' live from 1996 and an 'Acquiesce' music video.

At the time of the release, the CD boom was still in full swing and extended edition, special edition and limited-edition only tracks were ubiquitous. As such, there are some special features worth mentioning that are of particular interest to collectors and general fans alike. Most notably, a special edition of *Stop The Clocks* included not only an obligatory 32-page booklet but also a 40-minute mini-featurette titled 'Lock The Box', which is well worth watching and features great tidbits on every song. At Best Buy stores, the album was packaged with the *Stop The Clocks EP*, which contained 'Acquiesce', a demo version of 'Cigarettes & Alcohol', a live version from 1995 of 'Some Might Say' and 'The Masterplan'. There was also a promotion in which many copies featured a bonus DVD. Most surprising, perhaps, was the fact that the song 'Stop The Clocks' was not included on the compilation, it seemingly being the perfect opportunity to release it. Some have cited the song as being similar to 'Looking Glass' by The La's, and it had long been a song that people were aware of, having been written in 2011 and recorded during the sessions for the *Don't Believe The Truth* album. The song would eventually see official release on the first High Flying Birds album.

The cover of the album was designed by Sit Peter Blake, best known for designing the *Sgt. Pepper's Lonely Hearts Club Band* cover. The cover features familiar cultural artefacts and icons, adding to this notion of stopping time and reflecting. There was a mini semi-acoustic tour to promote this album, which yielded some interesting songs, among them, a great cover of 'Strawberry Fields Forever', which sounded fairly similar to the John Lennon demo of the song.

Singles 2007

'Lord Don't Slow Me Down' (N. Gallagher)

A-side single. Released: 21 October 2007. UK: 10

The first standalone, non-album single since 'Whatever' in 1994, this was also the first single not to reach the Top Four since 'Cigarettes & Alcohol' in 1994. Those numbers do not do the song justice, however, as this was a very good single from Oasis at this point in their career. A blues song infused with a dose of garage rock, or as Noel would describe it, 'one of the best things, like, The Who, The Yardbirds and the Jeff Beck Group combined...'. Recorded during the *Don't Believe The Truth* sessions, this song fits into the throwback nature of the album and would have been well-placed alongside most of the tracks.

Noel, however, had his reasons for removing it from the final track listing and it wound up as a bridge between the *Don't Believe The Truth* era and the *Dig Out Your Soul* era.

The lyrics are about life on the road, and it was quite the busy life for a couple of years in 2005 and 2006, in some ways the busiest touring years of their career. There is an unreleased studio version with Liam taking lead vocals – not for the first time, his voice suits the material better.

'The Meaning Of Soul (Live)' (L. Gallagher)

B-side single of 'Lord Don't Slow Me Down'

A fine song from *Don't Believe The Truth*, if not a slightly random choice for release as a B-side; at the time of this single's release, it had been recently used for Sky's Premier League coverage. Both this and the next track were culled from a very well-received City of Manchester Stadium gig in 2005.

'Don't Look Back In Anger (Live)' (N. Gallagher)

B-side single of 'Lord Don't Slow Me Down'

By 2005, 'Don't Look Back In Anger' had long ago become the biggest sing-along at any given Oasis concert, with only 'Live Forever' and 'Wonderwall' being in the same category. The song would take on even more meaning as a communal sing-along in the years after Oasis broke up. This is a terrific live version, with the audience acapella at the end being a highlight.

'Within You Without You' (G. Harrison)

Sgt. Pepper's Lonely Hearts Club Band 40th Anniversary Special on BBC Radio 2

In 2007, to mark the 40th anniversary of perhaps the most famous album in history, a variety of artists recreated all of the songs on *Sgt. Pepper's Lonely Hearts Club Band*, with the results then being broadcast on BBC Radio 2. Of course, Oasis were included in this slightly random assortment of artists and their choice of song was a bit surprising to some. For those familiar with *Standing On The Shoulder Of Giants,* the sound contained here was not much of a departure from some of those tracks.

Geoff Emerick, who engineered the original sessions in 1967, was in charge of the sessions here and one of the selling points of the project was that the original analogue four-track equipment was used. Perhaps the most notable part of Oasis's version is that the track opens up with the drums from 'Tomorrow Never Knows' as well as the tape loops, creating something of a mash-up. Lost a bit to history and one that won't make anyone forget the original, this track was an interesting footnote in 2007.

Dig Out Your Soul (2008)

Personnel:

Liam Gallagher: vocals

Noel Gallagher: electric and acoustic guitars, keyboards, electronics, drums (1, 3, 11), melodica (11), lead vocals (3, 6, 7)

Gem Archer: electric and acoustic guitars, keyboards, bass guitar

Andy Bell: bass guitar, electric guitar, keyboards, tamboura

Zak Starkey: drums

Jay Darlington: Mellotron, electronics (7)

The National In-Choir: backing vocals (2)

Produced and mixed by Dave Sardy

Recording engineers: Ryan Castle, Chris Bolster, Cameron Barton and Ghian Wright

Mastered by Ian Cooper

Pro Tools editing by Andy Brohard

Recorded in London between August 2007 and March 2008

UK release date: 6 October 2008

Chart placings: UK: 1, US: 5

2006 and 2007 were relatively quiet years for Oasis. Early 2006 saw them wrapping up their well-received *Don't Believe The Truth* tour, while the end of the year saw the release of the smashingly well-executed compilation *Stop The Clocks*. 2007 saw the release of the documentary *Lord Don't Slow Me Down* as well as the single of the same name, in addition to Noel playing some very well-received solo gigs throughout the year. No one knew it at the time, but 2008 would see the seventh and final Oasis studio album arriving in October of that year, released by Big Brother Recordings, but under the profit-sharing umbrella of Sony 'again'.

The first new music of 2008 that Noel Gallagher was attached to was 'Echoes Round The Sun' by Paul Weller, with Noel writing the rhythm section of the track and Gem also appearing on the track. Recordings for what would be *Dig Out Your Soul* began in 2007, with final mixing taking place in the first part of 2008. The first major Oasis news of 2008 involved a controversy that, in terms of notoriety, would be second only to the overhyped Blur vs Oasis drama of 1995 and Noel's comments about AIDS. As described elsewhere in this book under the 'Wonderwall' entry, Noel made some disparaging comments about Jay-Z headlining Glastonbury, which led to many Noel vs. Jay-Z headlines and 'Noel is an out-of-step rocker' clickbait articles. Jay-Z, to his credit, handled the controversy as well as anyone could, securing audio rights to the interview, which was played at Glastonbury and opening with 'Wonderwall'. Sales and streams of 'Wonderwall' spiked and everyone seemingly came out unscathed. Noel even got to make a few funny jokes about Jay-Z's use of a white Stratocaster. When Noel was asked how he felt about everything after the event, he said: 'It appears my opinions offend people. Well, stop asking me fucking questions then'.

Toss in a funny appearance that Liam had on *The F Word* that took up more headlines, and it became easy to forget that Oasis were, in fact, ready to release a new album into the world. Zak Starkey recorded drums for the new album but was not going to tour as a member of Oasis anymore, his time being taken up by a slew of other commitments. The first shows of 2008 were played stateside in August 2008 and featured four new songs from the upcoming album, including the first single, 'The Shock Of The Lightning'. When the single was eventually released in late September of 2008, it stalled at number three in the UK, which may seem admirable, but it was the first lead single since 'Supersonic' not to reach number one. Several reasons likely played into this: physical CD sales were tanking by 2008 and the only B-side on the single was a Chemical Brothers remix of 'Falling Down'. Oasis B-sides had been dipping in quality over the years, but to simply include a remix and no new music, or even a live version of a classic tune, was unprecedented. As with *Stop The Clocks*, there were so many deluxe versions released of *Dig Out Your Soul* that it became impossible to keep up once the album hit shelves on 6 October. As expected, the album hit number one, but reviews were mixed. Some said, like with *Don't Believe The Truth*, it was a return to form and their best work since 1995. Other outlets said it was their worst record, or at least equal to *Heathen Chemistry*. The tour to support the album was generally very well received and featured a setlist that was terrific, hitting almost every part of their career. Throughout the course of the tour, dozens of support acts came and went, with most reporting that Oasis were a terrific band to work with. The tour would become notable for being the last tour that the band would ever embark upon, some hints of which may have been present towards the end of 2008 when Noel began making disparaging comments towards Liam in his tour-diary blog, and the general change of attitude on stage. As 2009 began and the tour rolled on, rumours of the brothers travelling separately and simply not speaking at all began to emerge.

Noel struggled a bit with the album title, as he usually did. Admitting that Oasis albums may not have had the best titles in the past, he belaboured the decision. He considered naming the album 'Bag It Up' or 'The Shock Of The Lightning', but the fear of too much pressure being assigned to a title track convinced him otherwise. 'Standing On The Edge Of The Noise' was the next title he considered before settling on *Dig Out Your Soul*, which was, according to Noel, the best title on a day when he had to choose one. Specifically, the title alluded to a club DJ digging into his Motown records. What's more, Gem gave the suggestion – once again, a sign that Oasis was a more democratic band than ever before.

More so than with most bands, there always seems to be a story around a new Oasis single or album. Often, this is the result of comments made by the Gallagher brothers, unrealistic expectations by journalists or even a desire to see the band fail. The storylines can be interesting to sift through, but they mainly act as a distraction from the music – this was especially true with *Dig Out Your Soul*. Similar to *Don't Believe The Truth*, and even more so, the album is very top-heavy, with the best songs appearing on the first half of the record – this is also where most of Noel's songs were placed. The second half of the record leaves a lot to be desired and the last few songs, especially, are some of the worst of their career. Even so, most of their contemporaries had broken up or stopped releasing new music, while Oasis were still capable of writing a few terrific tunes. Their legacy will always be the music they made between 1994 and 1996, but *Dig Out Your Soul* is a worthy ending to one of the most impressive musical acts in history.

By May 2009, Noel gave an interview to *Q Magazine* that essentially confirmed all the rumours about his relationship with Liam:

> He's never seen my little lad, just pictures. To a stranger, it sounds ludicrous, but you wouldn't have him in the house if he spoke to you the way he speaks to me and my family. He's rude, arrogant, intimidating and lazy. He's the angriest man you'll ever meet. He's like a man with a fork in the world of soup.

Liam did nothing to dispel any of this, snapping back in his own way, mainly via Twitter, and so began the race to the end of Oasis, despite the classic Noel quote: 'I am Oasis. I'll never leave Oasis and Oasis will never leave me'. All came crashing to a halt, however, at the Rock en Seine festival in Paris, after already having to cancel a show due to Liam's voice. Oasis never made it on stage; there were rumours of a backstage fight and a guitar being smashed. Noel made his official statement the following morning:

> It's with some sadness and great relief to tell you that I quit Oasis tonight. People will write and say what they like, but I simply could not go on working with Liam a day longer... Apologies to all the people who bought tickets for the shows in Paris, Konstanz and Milan.

Over the years, more details would emerge as to why exactly Noel called it quits at that moment, but the seeds had been planted for several years prior. The magic between the brothers was equally volatile, and while both made some justified gripes, Noel finally snapped, and with him, Oasis.

'Bag It Up' (N. Gallagher)
Every Oasis album has typically opened with a Noel song, save for *Don't Believe The Truth*, and often a song that was also released as a single. This is a Noel song, to be sure, but 'Bag It Up' was not released as a single, although some may argue it should have been. Whether conscious or not, *Don't Believe The Truth* had a throwback sound, with many of the songs being directly and/or

indirectly influenced by groups that Oasis had cited as influences over the years. While there is a garage-rock undertone on 'Bag It Up', this is the first Oasis album opener that sounds of its time, which isn't necessarily a bad thing. There's a layered, big sound going on that will continue throughout the album, as *Dig Out Your Soul* is, without question, the heaviest Oasis album. 'Bag It Up' has a melody that won't quit, with lyrics and an overall vibe inspired by psychedelic drugs, including the idea that one can 'bag up' that feeling or mentality.

The lyrics are all over the place, in a fun way, with references to a cup of Lady Grey, the Monkey Man and 'freaks rising up through the floor'. The song was partly inspired by The Pretty Things song 'Baron Saturday', which they released in 1968. As the story goes, Serge Pizzomo from Kasabian played Noel the track, which compelled Noel to write a song just like it. Upon writing the song and titling it, he was unaware that Geri Halliwell of Spice Girls fame had a song with the same title. As one of the first three songs recorded for the album, all at Gem Archer's house, it became something of a blueprint for the album – the heavy, almost swamp-like vibe of the guitars permeates throughout. As Noel summarised to *Q Magazine*: 'slow pounding acid rock, The Pretty Things vs. The Pink Floyd on glue'. Never performed live, which is a shame, this latter-era highlight is a reminder of how great this band was, even at the end.

'The Turning' (N. Gallagher)

Another strong tune follows the rocking opener, many people citing this as a highlight from the record. While not as in-your-face as 'Bag It Up', 'The Turning' is heavy in its chorus and has a cascading lilt to the verses. Opening with a drumbeat, rare for an Oasis track, and being guided by a piano line, this is something of a return to a classic Oasis sound. Yet, the accompanying music when Liam sings, 'so come on, shake your rag doll, baby, before you change your mind', is almost industrial in nature, and wouldn't have sounded out of place on a Marilyn Manson album. More appropriately, it's heavy in the way that early Verve records were. The ending fades into a gentle guitar melody that sounds eerily like a 'Dear Prudence' outtake.

The rapture is mentioned here for the first time on the album, with Noel remarking that the lyrics were inspired by the world being at a critical point, close to snapping. Great lyrics and great Liam vocals – further proof that the first half of *Dig Out Your Soul* is a terrific album. Noel was onto something when he said this was The Stone Roses doing The Stooges.

'Waiting For The Rapture' (N. Gallagher)

Opening with one of the heaviest stomps in the Oasis catalogue, 'Waiting For The Rapture' initially sounds almost exactly like The Doors song 'Five To One'. That song, like this one, is a terrific blues-inspired romp. This is the first time Noel takes lead vocals on *Dig Out Your Soul*, and it makes sense given that the lyrics clearly seem to deal with Noel's girlfriend Sara MacDonald:

I still don't know what I was waiting for
A big love to fall down from the sky
She took my hand and picked me up off the floor
She put an apple in my eye

Andy Bell commented on Noel's ability to write lyrics: 'Noel can put things in a down-to-earth way that goes right to the core'. It's ironic that the music is so aggressive, given the sweet nature of the lyrics, with even the solo being one of the most aggressive in the Oasis canon. Noel penned six of the album's 11 tracks and takes lead vocals on three of them.

It's hard to hear, 'I bet you don't know about all that revolution in her head', and not think of 'Don't Look Back In Anger', which famously has Noel starting a revolution from his bed. To force a Beatles reference, 'Revolution In The Head' is also the title of one of the most infamous Beatles books of all time, one which Noel certainly read at some point.

'The Shock Of The Lightning' (N. Gallagher)
A-side single. Released: 29 September 2008 UK: 1
The highest charting single from *Dig Out Your Soul,* and for many, the best song on the album, as well as the last time that an Oasis single would appear in the Top Ten. 'The Shock Of The Lightning' is the most Oasis-sounding song on the album in that it sounds like something that could have been written ten years earlier. As with 'Waiting For The Rapture', fans assume that these lyrics relate to Noel's relationship with Sara MacDonald:

I'm all over my heart's desire
I feel cold but I'm back in the fire

The song arrives fast and furious with a buzzsaw-like sound, growing in volume. Written and recorded very quickly, Noel would say it is essentially the demo, retaining that same punk energy. Zak Starkey played drums on all but three *Dig Out Your Soul* tracks, with this being perhaps his best drumming on the album. One of the few Oasis songs to feature a drum solo (forward to about 3:20 for some inspired Starkey playing), this is perhaps the most propulsive song in the Oasis canon – it simply starts and doesn't let up. This is one of the few songs from the album that ever saw the light of a set list and it worked excellently live to the surprise of no one.

'I'm Outta Time' (L. Gallagher)
A-side single. Released: 1 December 2008. UK: 12
The first Liam song on the record and a clear highlight of the album. Liam had come a long way since the overly maligned 'Little James', and his songs were some of the minor highlights of the last three Oasis records. As was typical for Liam, this song is hugely inspired by John Lennon, going so far as

to include an excerpt from one of his last interviews, given in 1980. However, as the *NME* pointed out, a more apt comparison was likely The Verve, circa 'Urban Hymns'. The preceding four songs were all good/great, but the album needed a change of pace – 'I'm Outta Time' was the perfect choice to break up the album.

The black-and-white music video fits the atmospheric vibe of the song perfectly and simply features Liam journeying through an English landscape. Noel perhaps described the song best when he named it 'deceptively brilliant'. Peaking at number 12, this was the first Oasis single to miss the Top Ten since 1994's 'Shakermaker'.

Back to John Lennon. Most of the comparisons to Liam's hero, as it pertains to this song, come down to two things. First, at the end of the music video, Liam is seen, in a close-up profile, lying down in a way that almost mirrors the cover of Lennon's 1973 offering *Mind Games*. Second, and more obvious, the ending of 'I'm Outta Time' features a short speech excerpt from a John Lennon interview in which he says:

As Churchill said, it's every Englishman's inalienable right to live where the hell he likes. What's it going to do, vanish? Is it not going to be there when I get back?

In September 1971, John Lennon and Yoko Ono moved to the US, and Lennon would famously never return. Tragically, shortly after that interview from 1980, Lennon was shot and killed and never made it back to England. Liam perhaps chose this excerpt to show how Lennon was out of time. The song ends with a musical box playing and then fading out, creating one of the most haunting exits in the Oasis songbook.

'(Get Off Your) High Horse Lady' (N. Gallagher)

This was originally demoed for *Heathen Chemistry* but held back until *Dig Out Your Soul*, perhaps in an effort for Noel to have more songs on the album. While flashes of brilliance still remained, few could argue that Noel was writing at the same pace or consistency as he used to. Proof of that was in the songwriting credits to *Dig Out Your Soul*, *Don't Believe The Truth* and *Heathen Chemistry*. Of the 33 songs on those regular studio releases, and not counting the hidden track 'The Cage', Noel wrote 17 of those, which is barely half. The best songs from those albums and associated B-sides tended to be Noel songs, but the band had become significantly more democratic. This was not always a bad thing, as Liam, Gem and Andy were capable of writing a solid tune, but when songs like this were being dug up from past sessions to fill space on the new album, it was hard not to question Noel and where his muse had gone.

Another Noel lead vocal, which is significantly more effects-laden than usual, there is a bluesy, almost Western vibe to the song that makes this a

relative anomaly in the Oasis catalogue. There is a very laid-back quality to
the song, and with the lyrics essentially just repeating a few phrases, the track
gains power from its atypical Oasis sound. Certainly one of the lesser Noel
songs on the album, it works well as something of an unofficial mid-point to
the album.

'Falling Down' (N. Gallagher)
A-side single. Released: 9 March 2009. UK: 10
If the preceding track serves as the unofficial mid-point, this serves as the
very unofficial end to the album, as all but the most ardent of fans have
forgotten the four songs that follow. The last proper single that Oasis would
ever release during their time as a band, 'Falling Down', like 'I'm Outta Time',
failed to go any higher than the Top Ten in the UK, this time stalling right
at number ten. It was at least paired with a new song, 'Those Swollen Hand
Blues', of which there are both fans and detractors. Noel would refer to this
as his 'krautpop' song, saying it is the type of song that he had been wanting
to write for years.

Noel was, of course, always prone to exaggeration and would often over-
laud songs when they first came out before taking back his comments. True
to form, he had some strong words for 'Falling Down', saying it was one of
the best he had written in a very long time and felt it was fitting as the band's
final single. The lyrics are terrific, invoking a sense of feeling a distance
from your own surroundings and realising, perhaps, that we as people are
insignificant in the grand plans of the universe. It is somewhat surprising
that more fans and critics don't talk about the song in more glowing terms,
as it is one of the stronger Oasis tunes from the noughties. Of extra special
attention here is the instrumentation throughout the song, especially Starkey's
drums, with the patterns he is playing not far removed from 'Tomorrow Never
Knows'. The strings, the layered guitars and the percussion all work together
to create a swirling atmosphere within the song that feels like a spiralling
downward motion. Hardcore fans of the song will want to track down the
22-minute remix version by The Amorphous Androgynous, available on
YouTube. It's overkill, but it's fun.

The journey from their first single, 'Supersonic', to this, their last single, was
an impressive one:

> If I was to sit here now and listen to 'Supersonic' as the first and 'Falling
> Down' as the last, I'd think, 'well, that's a fuckin' pretty good journey, that
> is, between those two'. The songs are shit in between, but to bookend your
> career with those two – that'll do me.

'To Be Where There's Life' (G. Archer)
The biggest knock on *Dig Out Your Soul* is that Noel should have taken over
full songwriting duties, save for 'I'm Outta Time', which was well-received by

fans. The front half of the album is Noel-dominated and works better than the second half of the album. Not that the second half is bad, per se, but there is a noticeable drop in quality when Noel is not penning the songs. Where the non-Noel songs worked terrifically on *Don't Believe The Truth*, that was not always the case here. Those criticisms aside, the weakest songs on the album are the last three, which absolves this one, at least for the most part. Give the band credit for trying something a little different.

'To Be Where There's Life' is Gem's only songwriting credit on the album, down from having two songwriting credits on *Don't Believe The Truth*, plus composing the B-side 'Eyeball Tickler'. Musically, the most notable aspect of the song is the unique instrumentation; awash in droning sitars and bongos, it is a marked departure from most Oasis songs, harkening back a little to *Standing On The Shoulder Of Giants*. The song is a bassline with a drum groove, no guitars. Liam turns in a great vocal performance, especially following the instrumental breakdown at 3:00 when Liam comes back in, singing the line that gave the album its title: 'Dig out your soul, 'cause here we go'. Somewhat surprisingly, this song was featured in almost every show of the *Dig Out Your Soul* tour, and while it worked just fine, it's hard not to wish they played more of the Noel tracks instead.

'Ain't Got Nothin'' (L. Gallagher)
The equivalent of Liam's other short shot of piss and vinegar, 'The Meaning Of Soul', but for *Dig Out Your Soul*, this serves the same purpose here – it is fast and ferocious. In the words of Gem Archer, 'Liam wanted it to sound like The Who with Ginger Baker on drums, playing while a fight was happening'. The quote is fitting, as the song was inspired by Liam's 2002 fight in Munich in which he lost two of his teeth, specifically, Liam's upset with how the fight was reported in terms of who started it, who ended and who helped Liam:

They got nothing on me anymore
They got nothing on you
I don't care what they say anymore
All I want is the truth

Of course, there is a John Lennon track titled 'Gimme Some Truth', which, while perhaps a reach, could have been an inspiration for Liam on this one. Liam wrote this about six months after the fight occurred and sat on it until the sessions for *Dig Out Your Soul*. While certainly not a highlight, it's short enough not to cause too much of a fuss.

'The Nature Of Reality' (A. Bell)
Written by bass player Andy Bell, this is tucked away on side two of *Dig Out Your Soul*. Andy Bell's contributions to *Don't Believe The Truth* are some of the highlights of the record, but here, we are left with a track that is fine,

but forgettable. Noel provides excellent guitar work and Gem plays a groovy bassline. Andy Bell, on the other hand, did not appear on the song, instead wanting to provide guidance and feedback from the control room.

The most personal song that Andy Bell would ever write while in Oasis, the lyrics deal with his life in the aftermath of a divorce, and therapy that led him to become an atheist by way of Richard Dawkins' *The God Delusion*:

> Belief does not existence make
> It's only in your mind

While there are some interesting ideas lyrically, the song plods along musically and ends up feeling like one of the longest songs of this era, despite being under four minutes long.

'Soldier On' (L. Gallagher)
Being the last song on the last Oasis album certainly gives this song more symbolic depth with the benefit of hindsight. There is a fun story that Noel tells of how the song came to be on the album. The Coral recorded an album at Noel's studio, and they came across a hard drive that contained this song as part of a batch titled 'New Oasis Stuff'. Singer James Skelly turned to Noel and asked if they were going to record the track. Noel had no idea it even existed and the next thing he knew, Andy Bell had already recorded it with Liam. There are not many actual lyrics in the song, with the words 'soldier on' taking up the last half of the song. While in past years, this would have been relegated to B-side status or even stayed hidden on the hard drive, there is a poetic quality to having this track as the finale on *Dig Out Your Soul*, as Noel would write:

> It would have been easier, and more obvious, to put an uplifting song at the end of the album. When I hear 'Soldier On', I imagine a guy with a big fucking rope and a lump of concrete on his back, as if someone has told him, 'Right – there's your baggage, take it through your life'. That's why it was last on the album. I really, really love that song.

Dig Out Your Soul B-Sides/EPs
'Falling Down (Chemical Brothers Remix)' (N. Gallagher)
B-side single of 'The Shock Of The Lightning'
Noel has had a notable relationship with the musical duo The Chemical Brothers since their critically lauded 'Setting Sun' in 1996. The 1996 song, which Noel co-wrote with duo members Tom Rowlands and Ed Simons, proved to be one of the most acclaimed of his career. It was a number-one single in the UK and was included as one of the 200 Greatest Dance Songs of All Time by *Rolling Stone* magazine.

This single is the first Oasis song to include a remix on any type of studio release, not counting the promo-only version of the Lynchmob Beats Mix of

'Champagne Supernova'. This, then, becomes the first official single release that does not contain a new track as a B-side. While enjoyable and featuring some effect-heavy Noel vocal and keyboard tricks, it is likely not going to make many playlists. The Japanese edition of the single featured a Jagz Kooner remix of the song.

'I'm Outta Time (Twiggy Ramirez Remix)' (L. Gallagher)

B-side single of 'I'm Outta Time'

The 'I'm Outta Time' single was released in so many versions that it would be impossible to keep up with said versions and all the associated remixes. Twiggy Ramirez was best known for his association with shock-rocker Marilyn Manson. What he does with 'I'm Outta Time' ends up working relatively well, as he is not trying to reinvent the wheel. He keeps his remix pretty close to the original and it winds up as one of the most enjoyable remixes from the era.

'The Shock Of The Lightning (Jagz Kooner Remix)' (N. Gallagher)

B-side single of 'I'm Outta Time'

Jagz Kooner is back with another remix, this time of 'The Shock Of The Lightning', again staying closer to the original than one would expect from a remix.

'Those Swollen Hand Blues' (N. Gallagher)

B-side single of 'Falling Down'

There was really only one *true* B-side released during the *Dig Out Your Soul* era: 'Those Swollen Hand Blues'. The rest of the B-sides are simply remixes.

Several times throughout his career, Noel Gallagher has mentioned his love of the Pink Floyd song 'Nobody Home', an album track from *The Wall*. The song, essentially a Roger Waters solo track, speaks of isolation, despair and a general sense of aloneness. During a radio conversation, talking on 'Desert Island Discs', Noel Gallagher talks about his love of 'Nobody Home' and *The Wall*:

> ...I know every single word and I can sing it in sequence at the drop of a hat. Roger Waters, for me... I'd love to meet him. His songwriting is so simple, yet the story is so grandiose and the whole thing is so epic – I wish I could write an album like that, y'know. A concept album. I think I'd have to get extremely pretentious first, but this track, called 'Nobody Home', bends my head.

This B-side is named after the line in 'Nobody Home' in which our narrator states he 'got those swollen-hand blues'. This song was written and recorded during the *Don't Believe The Truth* sessions but was kept off the album and relegated to the 'Falling Down' single as the last proper Oasis B-side. The

'Falling Down' single includes three versions of said song, and then 'Those Swollen Hand Blues'. The days of singles full of amazing B-sides were in the distant past. While some may call this a throwaway track, the Beatles influence is palpable and it's a change of pace from most of the other songs in the Oasis catalogue. It was also nice to hear a non-album original from Noel on a single again.

'Falling Down (The Gibb Mix)' (N. Gallagher)
B-side single of 'Falling Down'
A very bass-heavy version of 'Falling Down'. The remixes are getting hard to keep up with.

'Falling Down (The Prodigy Version)' (N. Gallagher)
B-side single of 'Falling Down'
Oasis had a relationship with The Prodigy that peaked on the song 'Shoot Down', which appears on their 2004 album *Always Outnumbered, Never Outgunned*, but was recorded earlier. That song is a highlight of that record and is unlike anything else the Gallagher brothers had done. This remix has a very industrial undertone and is a departure from the studio version of 'Falling Down'. It ends up being one of the stronger remixes of the dozens from the era but has still been forgotten by most.

'Boy With The Blues' (L. Gallagher)
Ever since *Familiar To Millions* was released in a half-dozen different formats, there have been one-off special edition releases and promotional versions of singles that have made collecting Oasis music more complicated than it ever had to be. Sticking with the original UK albums and singles is the way to go, much like it is with The Beatles. This song was released as an iTunes exclusive EP in early July 2009, along with 'I Believe In All' and a Devendra Banhart remix of '(Get Off Your) High Horse Lady'. 'Boy With The Blues' was, again, released as part of a deluxe edition of *Dig Out Your Soul* and was also released on an *NCIS* soundtrack. On streaming services, as of the writing of this book, the *NCIS* soundtrack is the only place to hear this song.

Driven by a piano and acoustic guitar, this song would have fit perfectly on *Dig Out Your Soul* and it is a shame that it was not used as a B-side in lieu of one of the countless remixes. It has a major gospel vibe, with a fade-out that feels like it could go on as long as 'All Around The World'.

'I Believe In All' (L. Gallagher)
Released as a bonus track on the Japanese version and deluxe edition of *Dig Out Your Soul*. Another Liam composition, this is an energetic rocker and, like many of his other quick-hit songs, under three minutes. If any Oasis song is indicative of what Beady Eye would sound like, this is it. Like 'Boy With The Blues', it would have been nice to stumble across this tune as a B-side on one

of the three singles released from the album. Too similar to 'Ain't Got Nothin''
to be placed on *Dig Out Your Soul*, this is a fine Liam song but has been lost
to the complexities of the album's special editions and releases.

Time Flies...1994-2009

The premise of this 2010 compilation was very straightforward: to collect all 27 UK singles that Oasis released between 1994 and 2009. Notably, 'Whatever' and 'Lord Don't Slow Me Down' were included, which had previously never appeared on an Oasis studio album. Owing to Noel's dislike of the song, 'Sunday Morning Call' is not listed as a track but appears as a hidden track, following two minutes of silence after 'Falling Down' ends.

Released in a hurry in the wake of the end of Oasis, Sony put this out in the summer of 2010 to coincide with the 10th anniversary of *(What's the Story) Morning Glory?*. Oasis are one of the greatest singles bands of all time, and the compilation works very well, but there are a few gripes. The songs are not in chronological order and there's seemingly no rhyme or reason to the tracklisting. It would have made sense to list them chronologically, which also would have allowed fans to listen to the arc of their career. Secondly, by leaving off any and all non-singles, the compilation cannot be called comprehensive, as it leaves many of the band's greatest songs behind. Simply put, Oasis have too many good songs to fit onto two discs. Both *Stop The Clocks* and *Time Flies...1994-2009* are admirable, but you are better off with the original albums and singles or a curated playlist.

One Last Hurrah...

'Don't Stop...' (N. Gallagher)
A-side single. Released: 30 April 2020. UK: 80
The worldwide shutdown in spring 2020 due to the COVID-19 pandemic did carry with it at least one small victory for Oasis fans: Noel stumbled upon some 'new' Oasis music.

I've had infinite time to kill lately, so I thought I'd finally look and find out what was actually on the hundreds of faceless unmarked CDs I've got lying around at home. As fate would have it, I have stumbled across an old demo which I thought had been lost forever... Hope everyone is staying safe and trying to ride out the lockdown with a minimum of fuss. You're welcome, by the way.

Noel posted this on 29 April 2020, a day before the single was released. Until its release, 'Don't Stop...' was only known for being part of a soundcheck in Hong Kong from the early noughties, likely on the *Don't Believe The Truth* tour. It's a fine song, like most Noel acoustic ballads, and it was a pleasant surprise when Noel released it. *The Guardian*, perhaps a little too glowingly, declared it one of Noel Gallagher's best latter-day efforts. The most exciting part of the release, at least for those in the media, was likely the comments that Liam made. In response, Liam tweeted something along the lines of: don't bother releasing songs if Liam is not singing and Bonehead is not playing guitar. He also claimed that Noel overdubbed the song to give it more of a raw feel. The drama never ends and likely never will.

Knebworth 1996 (2021)

Personnel:
Liam Gallagher: lead vocals, tambourine
Noel Gallagher: lead guitar, vocals
Paul Arthurs: rhythm guitar
Paul McGuigan: bass guitar
Alan White: drums
UK release date: 19 November 2021
Chart placings: UK: 4, US: Did not chart

Not much new to say about this one. Their iconic Knebworth show(s) were combined to make a documentary and a live album. Interestingly, it was the highest-grossing documentary of 2021 in the UK. Notably, 'My Big Mouth' and 'It's Gettin' Better (Man!!)' were included in the setlist, albeit sandwiched between their two most beloved songs, which goes to show that Noel was somehow ready with the songs for a third album during this most tumultuous of years for the band.

As of this writing, this is the last officially released Oasis music, but expect a deluge of deluxe reissues and assorted expanded editions in the coming years.

Epilogue

While Oasis played their last concert together in August 2009, the dust refuses to settle as we approach 15 years since the Gallagher brothers last shared a stage. In a nutshell, Oasis managed to penetrate the British psyche and, as a result, have become permanently ingrained into British culture. *Definitely Maybe* and *(What's The Story) Morning Glory?* are two of the most popular albums of all time in the UK, with the songs therein continuing to top all sorts of lists. The accolades around those first two albums continue to grow at an almost absurd rate, 'not that it is not at least somewhat justifiable', as do the streams for 'Wonderwall', which is currently among the 100 most-streamed songs ever and the single most streamed song of the 1990s. *Definitely Maybe* has continually been ranked as the best album of all time by publications such as *NME* and *Q Magazine*. Never faring quite as well in America, even *Rolling Stone* still recognises it on its list of the 500 Greatest Albums of All Time.

A mere six months after the band split, Oasis won the Best British Album of the Last 30 years – for *(What's The Story) Morning Glory?* – at the 2010 Brit Awards. Notably, while accepting the award, Liam thanks Bonehead, Guigsy, Alan White and the fans, but not Noel. Liam proceeded to throw both his microphone and the award into the crowd, saying he thought it was a nice gesture to give the award to the fans. Liam could still garner headlines, with or without Noel.

Both brothers would continue making music, which was not really a surprise to anyone, they just would not be with each other. No one thought for a minute that a songwriter of Noel's calibre would stop writing and performing, and Liam was simply too good of a singer, too drawn to the limelight and the crowds to give that up. Liam, in fact, was up and running with a new band in 2010 called Beady Eye. Beady Eye featured every member who was part of the latest incarnation of Oasis, save for Noel. Their debut album *Different Gear, Still Speeding* was released in February 2011 to mixed reviews, although any excuse to have Liam still fronting a band was worth it. Beady Eye released another album, *BE*, in 2013, before disbanding the following year due to a variety of factors. Liam continued as a very successful solo artist and has released three records, all of which have gone to number one in the UK. As of this writing, his most recent concert had a 16-song setlist; 10 of those songs were Oasis tunes, despite Beady Eye initially not playing any Oasis music.

Noel went on to form Noel Gallagher's High Flying Birds and their self-titled debut was released in October 2011, which finally saw the release of the unreleased Oasis song 'Stop The Clocks'. Noel's debut was significantly more successful both critically and commercially than Beady Eye's, a fact not lost on journalists, who still wanted to put their names together in articles. Noel continues to release new music and tour under the High Flying Birds moniker, with all of his albums being well-received and even featuring some sonic experiments. As of this writing, Noel's most recent concert featured a 15-song setlist; 7 of those were Oasis songs, with the concert being broken into a first non-Oasis half and a second half that was essentially all Oasis tunes.

Between new albums and countless accolades for their old music, Oasis have never really disappeared from the news cycle, and coupled with both brothers' ability to steal headlines, Oasis are as ubiquitous as ever. There was even time to wrap up old headline-dominating feuds. March 2013 saw Noel and Damon sing the Blur's 'Tender' together on stage, with Paul Weller on drums. Both Damon and Noel would give touching quotes about the other in the aftermath of the performance and the two remain close friends. In May 2017, following an Ariana Grande concert at Manchester Arena, a suicide bomber detonated a homemade bomb which killed 23 and injured thousands. The ensuing weeks and months featured 'Don't Look Back In Anger' being sung at vigils, funerals and tribute concerts. In the process, this confirmed its status as something of a national anthem, more popular and canonical now than any Oasis song, save for maybe 'Live Forever'.

Unfortunately, the relationship between Liam and Noel appears to be at an all-time low, which is saying something. At this point, it seems as if Liam wants Oasis to reform and has said as much in interviews, although he has always loved to contradict himself. The main roadblock now seems to be Noel, who says he is making more money now than he ever did in the past and he has complete control over his albums, tours, songs and media appearances. At one point, Noel even said he would not reform Oasis, 'Not if all the starving children in the world depended on it'. But as of this writing, he has recently suggested that Liam 'has his number'. One will never quite know for sure what the brothers are actually thinking.

Oasis could never have ridden off into the sunset because they always burned too brightly for that. Their popularity was such that the only logical ending could have been that dramatic exit. And will they reform? The internet has a lot of guesses and plenty of articles have been written on the topic. The 30th anniversary of *Definitely Maybe* is in 2024 and *(What's The Story) Morning Glory?* celebrates that same anniversary the following year, which is to say that the time to strike would be now. But why? By catching a Liam show and a Noel show, you can hear what would approximate one relatively complete Oasis setlist. Equally relevant, there has been no shortage of Oasis content since the breakup, with the Gallagher brothers collectively releasing more music than was released during the lifetime of Oasis. 2016 saw the release of the excellent documentary *Oasis: Supersonic* and we have been treated to deluxe reissue treatments of the first three Oasis albums, with the rest of them likely on deck to get the deluxe treatment at some point. Noel's vaults are teeming with outtakes and untitled songs from the 1990s and noughties. We, as fans, will keep wondering and the brothers will keep getting asked. At least we have the songs to keep us company.

Bibliography

Essential Reading

Adams, Peter Richard and Matt Pooler., *Britpop* (Sonicbond Publishing, 2022).

Bowes, R., *Some Might Say: The Definitive Story Of Oasis* (This Day In Music Books, 2020).

Hewitt, Paolo., *Getting High: The Adventures Of Oasis* (Dean Street Press, 2015).

McCarroll, Tony., *Oasis: The Truth: My Life As Oasis's Drummer* (John Blake Books, 2012).

Niven, Alex., *Definitely Maybe (33⅓)* (Bloomsbury Academic, 2014).

Oasis, *Supersonic: The Complete, Authorised and Uncut Interviews* (Headline Books, 2021).

Online Resources

monobrowdemos.wordpress.com – Great website with information on demo versions of Oasis songs.

oasis-recordinginfo.co.uk – Terrific website containing a plethora of information on the early Oasis records, including interviews with those involved.

Visual and Audio Resources

Lord Don't Slow Me Down, directed by Ballie Walsh (Black Dog Films, 2007).

Oasis: Supersonic, directed by Mat Whitecross (Entertainment One, 2016).

Oasis: There We Were...Now Here We Are, directed by Dick Carruthers (Viacom, 2004).

The Oasis Podcast.

On Track series
Allman Brothers Band – Andrew Wild 978-1-78952-252-5
Tori Amos – Lisa Torem 978-1-78952-142-9
Aphex Twin – Beau Waddell 978-1-78952-267-9
Asia – Peter Braidis 978-1-78952-099-6
Badfinger – Robert Day-Webb 978-1-878952-176-4
Barclay James Harvest – Keith and Monica Domone 978-1-78952-067-5
Beck – Arthur Lizie 978-1-78952-258-7
The Beatles – Andrew Wild 978-1-78952-009-5
The Beatles Solo 1969-1980 – Andrew Wild 978-1-78952-030-9
Blue Oyster Cult – Jacob Holm-Lupo 978-1-78952-007-1
Blur – Matt Bishop 978-178952-164-1
Marc Bolan and T.Rex – Peter Gallagher 978-1-78952-124-5
Kate Bush – Bill Thomas 978-1-78952-097-2
Camel – Hamish Kuzminski 978-1-78952-040-8
Captain Beefheart – Opher Goodwin 978-1-78952-235-8
Caravan – Andy Boot 978-1-78952-127-6
Cardiacs – Eric Benac 978-1-78952-131-3
Nick Cave and The Bad Seeds – Dominic Sanderson 978-1-78952-240-2
Eric Clapton Solo – Andrew Wild 978-1-78952-141-2
The Clash – Nick Assirati 978-1-78952-077-4
Elvis Costello and The Attractions – Georg Purvis 978-1-78952-129-0
Crosby, Stills and Nash – Andrew Wild 978-1-78952-039-2
Creedence Clearwater Revival – Tony Thompson 978-178952-237-2
The Damned – Morgan Brown 978-1-78952-136-8
Deep Purple and Rainbow 1968-79 – Steve Pilkington 978-1-78952-002-6
Dire Straits – Andrew Wild 978-1-78952-044-6
The Doors – Tony Thompson 978-1-78952-137-5
Dream Theater – Jordan Blum 978-1-78952-050-7
Eagles – John Van der Kiste 978-1-78952-260-0
Earth, Wind and Fire – Bud Wilkins 978-1-78952-272-3
Electric Light Orchestra – Barry Delve 978-1-78952-152-8
Emerson Lake and Palmer – Mike Goode 978-1-78952-000-2
Fairport Convention – Kevan Furbank 978-1-78952-051-4
Peter Gabriel – Graeme Scarfe 978-1-78952-138-2
Genesis – Stuart MacFarlane 978-1-78952-005-7
Gentle Giant – Gary Steel 978-1-78952-058-3
Gong – Kevan Furbank 978-1-78952-082-8
Green Day – William E. Spevack 978-1-78952-261-7
Hall and Oates – Ian Abrahams 978-1-78952-167-2
Hawkwind – Duncan Harris 978-1-78952-052-1
Peter Hammill – Richard Rees Jones 978-1-78952-163-4
Roy Harper – Opher Goodwin 978-1-78952-130-6

Jimi Hendrix – Emma Stott 978-1-78952-175-7
The Hollies – Andrew Darlington 978-1-78952-159-7
Horslips – Richard James 978-1-78952-263-1
The Human League and The Sheffield Scene –
Andrew Darlington 978-1-78952-186-3
The Incredible String Band – Tim Moon 978-1-78952-107-8
Iron Maiden – Steve Pilkington 978-1-78952-061-3
Joe Jackson – Richard James 978-1-78952-189-4
Jefferson Airplane – Richard Butterworth 978-1-78952-143-6
Jethro Tull – Jordan Blum 978-1-78952-016-3
Elton John in the 1970s – Peter Kearns 978-1-78952-034-7
Billy Joel – Lisa Torem 978-1-78952-183-2
Judas Priest – John Tucker 978-1-78952-018-7
Kansas – Kevin Cummings 978-1-78952-057-6
The Kinks – Martin Hutchinson 978-1-78952-172-6
Korn – Matt Karpe 978-1-78952-153-5
Led Zeppelin – Steve Pilkington 978-1-78952-151-1
Level 42 – Matt Philips 978-1-78952-102-3
Little Feat – Georg Purvis - 978-1-78952-168-9
Aimee Mann – Jez Rowden 978-1-78952-036-1
Joni Mitchell – Peter Kearns 978-1-78952-081-1
The Moody Blues – Geoffrey Feakes 978-1-78952-042-2
Motorhead – Duncan Harris 978-1-78952-173-3
Nektar – Scott Meze – 978-1-78952-257-0
New Order – Dennis Remmer – 978-1-78952-249-5
Nightwish – Simon McMurdo – 978-1-78952-270-9
Laura Nyro – Philip Ward 978-1-78952-182-5
Mike Oldfield – Ryan Yard 978-1-78952-060-6
Opeth – Jordan Blum 978-1-78-952-166-5
Pearl Jam – Ben L. Connor 978-1-78952-188-7
Tom Petty – Richard James 978-1-78952-128-3
Pink Floyd – Richard Butterworth 978-1-78952-242-6
The Police – Pete Braidis 978-1-78952-158-0
Porcupine Tree – Nick Holmes 978-1-78952-144-3
Queen – Andrew Wild 978-1-78952-003-3
Radiohead – William Allen 978-1-78952-149-8
Rancid – Paul Matts 989-1-78952-187-0
Renaissance – David Detmer 978-1-78952-062-0
REO Speedwagon – Jim Romag 978-1-78952-262-4
The Rolling Stones 1963-80 – Steve Pilkington 978-1-78952-017-0
The Smiths and Morrissey – Tommy Gunnarsson 978-1-78952-140-5
Spirit – Rev. Keith A. Gordon – 978-1-78952- 248-8
Stackridge – Alan Draper 978-1-78952-232-7

Status Quo the Frantic Four Years – Richard James 978-1-78952-160-3
Steely Dan – Jez Rowden 978-1-78952-043-9
Steve Hackett – Geoffrey Feakes 978-1-78952-098-9
Tears For Fears – Paul Clark - 978-178952-238-9
Thin Lizzy – Graeme Stroud 978-1-78952-064-4
Tool – Matt Karpe 978-1-78952-234-1
Toto – Jacob Holm-Lupo 978-1-78952-019-4
U2 – Eoghan Lyng 978-1-78952-078-1
UFO – Richard James 978-1-78952-073-6
Van Der Graaf Generator – Dan Coffey 978-1-78952-031-6
Van Halen – Morgan Brown – 9781-78952-256-3
The Who – Geoffrey Feakes 978-1-78952-076-7
Roy Wood and the Move – James R Turner 978-1-78952-008-8
Yes – Stephen Lambe 978-1-78952-001-9
Frank Zappa 1966 to 1979 – Eric Benac 978-1-78952-033-0
Warren Zevon – Peter Gallagher 978-1-78952-170-2
10CC – Peter Kearns 978-1-78952-054-5

Decades Series
The Bee Gees in the 1960s – Andrew Mon Hughes et al 978-1-78952-148-1
The Bee Gees in the 1970s – Andrew Mon Hughes et al 978-1-78952-179-5
Black Sabbath in the 1970s – Chris Sutton 978-1-78952-171-9
Britpop – Peter Richard Adams and Matt Pooler 978-1-78952-169-6
Phil Collins in the 1980s – Andrew Wild 978-1-78952-185-6
Alice Cooper in the 1970s – Chris Sutton 978-1-78952-104-7
Alice Cooper in the 1980s – Chris Sutton 978-1-78952-259-4
Curved Air in the 1970s – Laura Shenton 978-1-78952-069-9
Donovan in the 1960s – Jeff Fitzgerald 978-1-78952-233-4
Bob Dylan in the 1980s – Don Klees 978-1-78952-157-3
Brian Eno in the 1970s – Gary Parsons 978-1-78952-239-6
Faith No More in the 1990s – Matt Karpe 978-1-78952-250-1
Fleetwood Mac in the 1970s – Andrew Wild 978-1-78952-105-4
Fleetwood Mac in the 1980s – Don Klees 978-178952-254-9
Focus in the 1970s – Stephen Lambe 978-1-78952-079-8
Free and Bad Company in the 1970s – John Van der Kiste 978-1-78952-178-8
Genesis in the 1970s – Bill Thomas 978178952-146-7
George Harrison in the 1970s – Eoghan Lyng 978-1-78952-174-0
Kiss in the 1970s – Peter Gallagher 978-1-78952-246-4
Manfred Mann's Earth Band in the 1970s – John Van der Kiste 978178952-243-3
Marillion in the 1980s – Nathaniel Webb 978-1-78952-065-1
Van Morrison in the 1970s – Peter Childs - 978-1-78952-241-9
Mott the Hoople and Ian Hunter in the 1970s –
John Van der Kiste 978-1-78-952-162-7

Pink Floyd In The 1970s – Georg Purvis 978-1-78952-072-9
Suzi Quatro in the 1970s – Darren Johnson 978-1-78952-236-5
Queen in the 1970s – James Griffiths 978-1-78952-265-5
Roxy Music in the 1970s – Dave Thompson 978-1-78952-180-1
Slade in the 1970s – Darren Johnson 978-1-78952-268-6
Status Quo in the 1980s – Greg Harper 978-1-78952-244-0
Tangerine Dream in the 1970s – Stephen Palmer 978-1-78952-161-0
The Sweet in the 1970s – Darren Johnson 978-1-78952-139-9
Uriah Heep in the 1970s – Steve Pilkington 978-1-78952-103-0
Van der Graaf Generator in the 1970s – Steve Pilkington 978-1-78952-245-7
Rick Wakeman in the 1970s – Geoffrey Feakes 978-1-78952-264-8
Yes in the 1980s – Stephen Lambe with David Watkinson 978-1-78952-125-2

On Screen series
Carry On... – Stephen Lambe 978-1-78952-004-0
David Cronenberg – Patrick Chapman 978-1-78952-071-2
Doctor Who: The David Tennant Years – Jamie Hailstone 978-1-78952-066-8
James Bond – Andrew Wild 978-1-78952-010-1
Monty Python – Steve Pilkington 978-1-78952-047-7
Seinfeld Seasons 1 to 5 – Stephen Lambe 978-1-78952-012-5

Other Books
1967: A Year In Psychedelic Rock 978-1-78952-155-9
1970: A Year In Rock – John Van der Kiste 978-1-78952-147-4
1973: The Golden Year of Progressive Rock 978-1-78952-165-8
Babysitting A Band On The Rocks – G.D. Praetorius 978-1-78952-106-1
Eric Clapton Sessions – Andrew Wild 978-1-78952-177-1
Derek Taylor: For Your Radioactive Children –
Andrew Darlington 978-1-78952-038-5
The Golden Road: The Recording History of The Grateful Dead – John Kilbride 978-1-78952-156-6
Iggy and The Stooges On Stage 1967-1974 – Per Nilsen 978-1-78952-101-6
Jon Anderson and the Warriors – the road to Yes –
David Watkinson 978-1-78952-059-0
Magic: The David Paton Story – David Paton 978-1-78952-266-2
Misty: The Music of Johnny Mathis – Jakob Baekgaard 978-1-78952-247-1
Nu Metal: A Definitive Guide – Matt Karpe 978-1-78952-063-7
Tommy Bolin: In and Out of Deep Purple – Laura Shenton 978-1-78952-070-5
Maximum Darkness – Deke Leonard 978-1-78952-048-4
The Twang Dynasty – Deke Leonard 978-1-78952-049-1

and many more to come!

Would you like to write for Sonicbond Publishing?
At Sonicbond Publishing we are always on the look-out for authors, particularly for our two main series:

On Track. Mixing fact with in depth analysis, the On Track series examines the work of a particular musical artist or group. All genres are considered from easy listening and jazz to 60s soul to 90s pop, via rock and metal.

On Screen. This series looks at the world of film and television. Subjects considered include directors, actors and writers, as well as entire television and film series. As with the On Track series, we balance fact with analysis.

While professional writing experience would, of course, be an advantage the most important qualification is to have real enthusiasm and knowledge of your subject. First-time authors are welcomed, but the ability to write well in English is essential.

Sonicbond Publishing has distribution throughout Europe and North America, and all books are also published in E-book form. Authors will be paid a royalty based on sales of their book.

Further details are available from www.sonicbondpublishing.co.uk. To contact us, complete the contact form there or
email info@sonicbondpublishing.co.uk